Dr. Flis has been an educator for over 18 years. He has taught high school students with special needs and typical students both inside and outside of the public-school setting. He received his Ed. D. in organizational leadership with an emphasis in special education in 2020 from Grand Canyon University in Phoenix, Arizona. He also holds a M.Ed. in curriculum and instruction from Arizona State University, Scottsdale, Arizona, and an B.A. in international studies from University of South Florida, Tampa, Florida. Dr. Flis enjoys aviation and holds a FAA Commercial Pilot Certificate and FAA Instructors Certificate. He has a State of Arizona Teaching Certificate in special education with a cross-categorical endorsement.

Dr. Flis also resided in Brazil for over 20 years and was owner of a marine agency and telecommunications business in Vitoria-ES, Brazil. The company had 18 fulltime employees. Currently, he lives in Tucson, Arizona, and enjoys the mountains and desert climate. His philosophy of education is that all students are different and must have a motivating educational environment where they can grow emotionally, mentally, physically, and socially. He endeavors to create this type of atmosphere where learners can meet their full potential. It is his wish to provide a safe environment where students are invited to share their ideas and learn from their mistakes.

I dedicate this book to fellow educators with whom I work with and who teach special needs students in general and self-contained classroom settings.

Clem Flis

An Educator's Handbook of Student Disorders

AUSTIN MACAULEY PUBLISHERS™
LONDON * CAMBRIDGE * NEW YORK * SHARJAH

Copyright © Clem Flis 2023

All rights reserved. No part of this publication may be reproduced, distributed, or transmitted in any form or by any means, including photocopying, recording, or other electronic or mechanical methods, without the prior written permission of the publisher, except in the case of brief quotations embodied in critical reviews and certain other non-commercial uses permitted by copyright law. For permission requests, write to the publisher.

Any person who commits any unauthorized act in relation to this publication may be liable to criminal prosecution and civil claims for damages.

This is a work of fiction. Names, characters, businesses, places, events, locales, and incidents are either the products of the author's imagination or used in a fictitious manner. Any resemblance to actual persons, living or dead, or actual events is purely coincidental.

Ordering Information
Quantity sales: Special discounts are available on quantity purchases by corporations, associations, and others. For details, contact the publisher at the address below.

Publisher's Cataloging-in-Publication data
Flis, Clem
An Educator's Handbook of Student Disorders

ISBN 9781685620806 (Paperback)
ISBN 9781685620813 (ePub e-book)

Library of Congress Control Number: 2023905048

www.austinmacauley.com/us

First Published 2023
Austin Macauley Publishers LLC
40 Wall Street, 33rd Floor, Suite 3302
New York, NY 10005
USA

mail-usa@austinmacauley.com
+1 (646) 5125767

I would like to thank my colleagues and teachers who inspired me to write and publish this book.

Table of Contents

Preface	17
Introduction	18
Charts, Graphs, and Tables	19
Chapter 1: Attention Deficit Hyperactivity Disorder	20
Introduction	20
What is Attention Deficit Hyperactivity Disorder (ADHD)?	20
Characteristics/Traits	21
Comorbid Disabilities/Disorders	21
Treatments	22
Medications	22
Teaching Students with ADHD	22
Conclusions	23
Recommendations	23
Chapter 2: Autism Spectrum Disorder	25
Introduction	25
What is Autism Spectrum Disorder (ASD)?	25
Characteristics/Traits	26
Comorbid Disabilities/Disorders	27
Treatments	27
Medications	28
Teaching Students with ASD	28

Conclusions   *29*

Recommendations   *29*

Chapter 3: Bipolar Disorder   **30**

Introduction   *30*

What is Bipolar Disorder?   *30*

Characteristics/Traits   *31*

Comorbid Disabilities/Disorders   *31*

Treatments   *32*

Medications   *32*

Teaching Students with Bipolar Disorder   *33*

Conclusions   *33*

Recommendations   *34*

Chapter 4: Echolalia   **35**

Introduction   *35*

What is Echolalia?   *35*

Characteristics/Traits   *36*

Comorbid Disabilities/Disorders   *36*

Treatments   *36*

Medications   *37*

Teaching Students with Echolalia   *37*

Conclusions   *38*

Recommendations   *38*

Chapter 5: Emotional Disability   **40**

Introduction   *40*

What is Emotional Disability (ED)?   *40*

Characteristics/Traits   *41*

Comorbid Disabilities/Disorders   *41*

Treatments	*41*
Medications	*42*
Teaching Students with ED	*42*
Conclusions	*43*
Recommendations	*43*

Chapter 6: Fetal Alcohol Syndrome Disorder — **44**

Introduction	*44*
What is Fetal Alcohol Syndrome (FASD)?	*44*
Characteristics/Traits	*45*
Comorbid Disabilities/Disorders	*45*
Treatments	*45*
Medications	*46*
Teaching Students with FASD	*46*
Conclusions	*46*
Recommendations	*47*

Chapter 7: Hyperosmia — **48**

Introduction	*48*
What is Hyperosmia?	*48*
Characteristics/Traits	*49*
Comorbid Disabilities/Disorders	*49*
Treatments	*49*
Medications	*50*
Teaching Students with Hyperosmia	*50*
Conclusions	*51*
Recommendations	*51*

Chapter 8: Intellectual Disability (ID) — **52**

Introduction	*52*

What is an Intellectual Disability (ID)? 52
Characteristics/Traits 53
Comorbid Disabilities/Disorders 53
Treatments 53
Medications 54
Teaching Students with ID 54
Conclusions 55
Recommendations 55

Chapter 9: Learning Disability 56

Introduction 56
What is Learning Disability (LD)? 56
Characteristics/Traits 57
Comorbid Disabilities/Disorders 57
Treatments 57
Medications 58
Teaching Students with LD 58
Conclusions 59
Recommendations 59

Chapter 10: Misophonia 60

Introduction 60
What Is Misophonia? 60
Characteristics/Traits 61
Comorbid Disabilities/Disorders 61
Treatments 61
Medications 62
Teaching Students with Misophonia 62
Conclusions 63

Recommendations ... 63

Chapter 11: Obsessive-Compulsive Disorder ... 65

Introduction ... 65

What is Obsessive-Compulsive Disorder (OCD)? ... 65

Characteristics/Traits ... 66

Comorbid Disabilities/Disorders ... 66

Treatments ... 67

Medications ... 67

Teaching Students with OCD ... 67

Conclusions ... 68

Recommendations ... 68

Chapter 12: Oppositional Defiant Disorder ... 70

Introduction ... 70

What is Oppositional Defiant Disorder (ODD)? ... 70

Characteristics/Traits ... 71

Comorbid Disabilities/Disorders ... 71

Treatments ... 72

Medications ... 72

Teaching Students with ODD ... 73

Conclusions ... 73

Recommendations ... 74

Chapter 13: Photophobia ... 75

Introduction ... 75

What is Photophobia? ... 75

Characteristics/Traits ... 76

Comorbid Disabilities/Disorders ... 76

Treatments ... 76

    Medications   *77*

    Teaching Students with Photophobia   *77*

    Conclusions   *77*

    Recommendations   *78*

Chapter 14: Rett Syndrome   **79**

    Introduction   *79*

    What is Rett Syndrome?   *79*

    Characteristics/Traits   *80*

    Comorbid Disabilities/Disorders   *80*

    Treatment   *81*

    Medications   *81*

    Teaching Students with Rett Syndrome   *81*

    Conclusions   *82*

    Recommendations   *82*

Chapter 15: Schizophrenia   **83**

    Introduction   *83*

    What is Schizophrenia?   *83*

    Characteristics/Traits   *84*

    Comorbid Disabilities/Disorders   *85*

    Treatments   *85*

    Medications   *86*

    Teaching Students with Schizophrenia   *86*

    Conclusions   *87*

    Recommendations   *87*

Chapter 16: Self-Injurious Behavior   **88**

    Introduction   *88*

    What is Self-Injurious Behavior?   *88*

Characteristics/Traits	*89*
Comorbid Disabilities/Disorders	*89*
Treatments	*90*
Medications	*90*
Teaching Students with Self-Injurious Behavior	*90*
Conclusions	*91*
Recommendations	*91*
Chapter 17: Antisocial Personality Disorders	**92**
Introduction	*92*
What is an Antisocial Personality Disorder?	*92*
Characteristics/Traits	*93*
Comorbid Disabilities/Disorders	*93*
Treatments	*94*
Medications	*95*
Teaching Students with Social Pathology and Psychopathology	*95*
Conclusions	*96*
Recommendations	*96*
Chapter 18: Social Skills Deficit and Speech/Language Disorders	**97**
Introduction	*97*
What is a Social Skills Deficit?	*97*
What is a Speech/Language Disorder?	*98*
Characteristics/Traits	*98*
Comorbid Disabilities/Disorders	*99*
Treatments	*100*
Medications	*100*
Teaching Students with Social Skills Deficit and Speech/ Language Disorder	*100*

Conclusions	*101*
Recommendations	*101*
Chapter 19: Tourette's Syndrome	**103**
Introduction	*103*
What is Tourette's Syndrome?	*103*
Characteristics/Traits	*104*
Comorbid Disabilities/Disorders	*104*
Treatments	*105*
Medications	*105*
Teaching Students with Tourette's Syndrome	*105*
Conclusions	*106*
Recommendations	*106*
Summary	**108**
Glossary	**110**
References	**120**
Appendix	**133**
Section I. Approximate Locations of Parts of the Brain	*133*
Section II. List of Drugs Used to Treat Disabilities, Disorders, and Comorbidities	*134*
Indexs	**159**

Preface

After many years of teaching students in a self-contained classroom, there was a realization that educators need to have a better understanding of student disorders that may hinder their learning and progress. With a thorough understanding of the components of most student disorders, student learning will greatly influence through the application of appropriate educator strategies based on scientific evidence. Understanding characteristics or traits of disorders helps educators de-escalate inappropriate student behaviors and understand students' needs and desires. This will improve overall classroom management.

Because of this lack of understanding of student disorders, it was felt that a handbook of basic components of some of the most common student disorders and disabilities will help general educators, special educators, school administrators, and therapists. For these reasons, it was decided that an educators' handbook of classroom disorders will be extremely beneficial to both novice and experienced educators, school administrators, and therapists. This handbook is designed to serve as a guide for educators in the classroom, during professional development, and as a supplement to be used during certification courses at the university level. I hope this handbook will enhance your insight into the complexities of mental disorders and disabilities.

– Clement R. Flis Jr. Ed.D.

Introduction

Why can't Johnny sit still in his seat for more than a few minutes? Why does Sam engage in ritualistic behaviors and remain detached from reality and in his own world? How can I communicate with Jane when she repeats everything I ask her? These are some of many questions that will be answered in this handbook. These are the types of questions that are being asked by educators in schools across the country. The reason these questions are asked is due to lack of understanding of student disorders.

The problem is that there is lack of understanding of student disabilities and disorders. This lack of understanding exacerbates inappropriate behavior, student meltdowns, deficient classroom management, and below average learning and progress. The purpose of this book is to improve understanding of student disabilities and disorders. With better understanding, educators will be in an improved position to use appropriate strategies and routines to control student behaviors and improve student learning and progress based on scientific evidence. Every student is different and will respond differently to strategies and routines applied. Students react differently because of the differences in the characteristics and severities of disabilities and disorders manifested by the students.

This book is divided into 19 chapters that describe the most common disabilities and disorders students exhibit in the school classroom. The disabilities and disorders are broken down in the chapters to define and describe as follows: Disability or disorder, characteristics/traits, comorbid disabilities or disorders, treatments, medications, how to teach students, conclusions, and recommendations. The scope of this book is to focus on mental disabilities and disorders that hinder student learning and progress and not physical impairments. The reader must keep in mind that laws, treatments, medications change. What is relevant to a certain disability or disorder may change over time.

Charts, Graphs, and Tables

Approximate Locations of Parts of the Brain .... Chart, Appendix, Section One

List of Drugs Used to Treat Disabilities and Disorders .... Table, Appendix, Section Two

Chapter 1
Attention Deficit Hyperactivity Disorder

Introduction

This chapter will cover Attention Deficit Hyperactivity Disorder (ADHD). This disorder is a leading and very common disorder in public and private schools of all grade levels. It is important to understand ADHD characteristics, comorbid disabilities, and disorders that may accompany ADHD, treatments, and medication available, and how to teach students with this disorder. Educators should understand the above-mentioned components of ADHD to be able to experience less classroom disruption and realize higher student learning levels and more progress.

What is Attention Deficit Hyperactivity Disorder (ADHD)?

Attention deficit hyperactivity disorder is a syndrome found in children and adults that manifests developmentally unsuitable inattention, impulsive behavior, and hyperactivity that exhibits behavioral impairments at home, school, or workplace (Swanson et al., 2006). ADHD is a genetic disorder with indications from brain-imaging and neuropsychological studies that associate dopamine and norepinephrine transmitter structures in the frontostriatal part of the brain are related to disorderly physiological processes. Low weight at birth and environmental factors, including exposure to lead and head trauma, are related to the symptoms of ADHD (Rappley, 2005).

Characteristics/Traits

According to Brown (2009), acting without thinking, anger, anxiety, behavioral disorders, deadlines, depression, excessive talking, fidgeting, organization, problems paying attention, and short attention span are some of the characteristics manifested in children and adults with ADHD. These traits can hinder the learning and progress of students in school and be detrimental to success in the workplace. Educators must be aware and be ready to confront these challenges in their classrooms. In the workplace, managers must be aware and be able to aid employees who have ADHD. Traits of ADHD will very among different individuals.

Comorbid Disabilities/Disorders

Comorbidities associated with ADHD include Obsessive-Compulsive Disorder (OCD), Oppositional Defiant Disorder, Learning Disorder, Speech Language deficits, Fine and Gross Motor Deficits, and Executive Function Disorders. Behavioral disorder may develop later in life and leave the person more vulnerable to future psychotic disorders (Faraone et al., 2015). There is strong evidence that there is a correlation between ADHD and Asthma (Cortese et al., 2018). Like many other disorders, for individuals with ADHD, the conditions they manifest can be from mild to severe. Financial issues, automobile accidents, alcohol and drug abuse, and legal issues leading to arrest and jail time can afflict individuals with ADHD.

Studies indicate that ADHD is caused by many things including brain function, genes and heredity, fetal exposure to alcohol and smoking, and toxins in the environment (Durston, 2010). The part of the brain is the prefrontal cortex, and its connections affect ADHD. See Section I. of the Appendix for approximate location in the brain. Neural pathways may not properly connect, have a slower connection, or be impaired. This area manages attention, focus, organization, and routine tasks.

Treatments

ADHD can be treated, but because this disorder is genetic, it cannot be cured. The use of support groups can consist of individuals with the same disorder who are given the opportunity to share their experiences with ADHD. Anger management therapy is an approach to teach students to control their anger. Psychological counseling addresses family, school, social deficits, and the work environment. Including family members in the therapy will help them become aware of ADHD and solve issues arising from characteristics manifested by persons with this disorder. Using Applied Behavior Analysis can alleviate in appropriate behavior by understanding the antecedent causing the behavior, understanding the behavior, and lastly, the consequence arising from the behavior acted out. Therapies can be developed to replace the inappropriate behavior with another less severe or more appropriate behavior (Hechtman, 2016).

Medications

Norpramin, Tofranil, and Wellbutrin may be prescribed as primary treatment for ADHD. Some of the names of other medications prescribed are Adderall XR (amphetamine), Concerta (methylphenidate), Dexedrine (amphetamine), Evekeo (amphetamine), Focalin XR (dexmethylphenidate), Quillivant XR (methylphenidate), Ritalin (methylphenidate), and Strattera (atomoxetine hydrochloride) (Briars and Todd, 2016). See Section II. of the Appendix for List of Drugs with explanations of how they are used for treatment. These drugs are prescribed by mental healthcare specialists and are not intended to work equally well for all individuals. Some individuals may react more positively to one type of medication over another. Medications for mental disorder must be prescribed on an individualized basis.

Teaching Students with ADHD

Teaching students with any disability or disorder can be challenging both for the educator and the student. Following several steps listed below can help reduce challenges associated with teaching this population. Teaching using individualization is a key to successful learning. No two students are the same. Most special needs students with disorders already have an Individualized Education Plan (IEP) in place. It is important to get to know your students.

Educators must know the parents or caretakers of students. They must be aware of cultural diversities of the students. Educators must apply scientific-based methods when teaching. Using Applied Behavior Analysis helps with classroom management and progress of students. Understand how different students learn best. Some students are visual learners and others are tactile learners. Check out different learning styles online and apply the strategies associated with each of these learning styles. These learning styles are related to multiple intelligences.

Applying learning styles and multiple intelligence types of students can allow the students to recognize their strengths and weaknesses and learn from them. The Theory of Multiple Intelligences suggested by Gardner in the early 1980s was an alternative strategy to older classroom designs. There was a need use a variety of ways people learn and understand (Sabriye and Çokçalışkan, 2018). It is important to understand what students like, therefore; plan teaching around what the student likes. A student may not like to write but may be happy to write about subject that the student knows and likes. An example of this is video games.

Conclusions

It is suggested that educators understand the intricacies of this student disorder and how teaching strategies will hinder or enhance learning. It is important that educators know their student as well as their background, culture, and parents or caretakers. Having knowledge of the socio-economic level of the students is extremely important. Lastly, being able to apply evidence-based practices based on scientific theory will enhance student learning and progress. Being able to differentiate instruction based on the student disorder and student cognitive level while using evidence-based practices will help overcome the challenges educators have interacting with student with special needs. These teaching strategies will enhance students' progress and improve classroom management with fewer periods of inappropriate behavioral meltdowns.

Recommendations

Educators should learn about different student disabilities and disorders present in classrooms. It is especially important that general educators as well as special educators become familiar these student deficiencies as well. More and more special-needs students are attending regular classes in general education classroom settings. A thorough understanding of disorders, improved knowledge of evidence-based practices, and knowing the students' needs will enhance the overall learning and progress of both typical and atypical students. Educators should also be more aware of the medications that are taken by the students and if are continuously available and being properly taken.

Chapter 2
Autism Spectrum Disorder

Introduction

This chapter will cover Autism Spectrum Disorder (ASD). Autism Spectrum Disorder (ASD) refers to a broad range of neurodevelopmental disorders with characteristics of impaired speech-language, social skill deficits, occupational impairments, repetitive behaviors, interests, and activities (Dillon, Underwood, and Freemantle, 2016). ASD is one of the fastest growing genetic disorders and can be diagnosed months after birth. It is unknown what causes ASD. This disorder is four times more common in males than in females. This chapter will focus on what ASD is, its characteristics, comorbid disabilities and disorders associated with ASD, treatments, medications, teaching students with ASD, and conclusions.

What is Autism Spectrum Disorder (ASD)?

ASD is a genetic disorder and developmental disability. Diagnosis of ASD is based on the early onset of social, speech/language, repetitive behavior, and interests. These above components will vary with any cognitive ability making ASD diverse (Frith and Happé, 2005). Every person who has ASD exhibits different levels of this disorder. Students with high performing ASD can interact very well in social circles, do well in school, obtain university degrees, hold responsible jobs, and marry. Students with high performing ASD can also have behavioral issues and become disruptive in classrooms. Some people with ASD are gifted such as Albert Einstein (Grandin, 1995). On the other hand, students with profound and severe autism may be non-verbal, have motor skills deficits, unable to function in social circles, and may need life-long assistance with basic living skills. Many individuals with ASD regardless of the degree of severity can exhibit violent verbal and physical behavior.

It is unclear what causes ASD. Autism is inherited. Siblings have 50 times greater risk of having Autism than the general population. If the mother and father both possess recessive alleles, their offspring has a higher risk of having autism. There have been many studies indicating that vaccines, high levels of mercury, viruses, allergies, and gastric inflammation are responsible for causing ASD, but these studies have been disproven. Diet has also been suggested as a cause of autism. Up until now, there is no evidence that environmental pathogens cause ASD (Frith and Happé, 2005). Individuals with ASD have a hippocampus with reduced size. This is the part of the brain responsible for the storage of memory.

Characteristics/Traits

Many preschool children with ASD exhibit no awareness of other children, they choose not to make friends. They may be confused by the actions of typical students and show no empathy. Higher performing students with ASD may seek the attention of adults, may speak correct but manifest stilted or awkward manager. These students may have strong obsessions with trains, vacuum cleaners, or other mechanical devices. They do not like changes in daily routines; these changes may cause meltdowns. In school, if asked to complete an assignment or change an activity, these students may become disruptive and oppositional. Other times, they will remain unfocused concentrating on a repetitive or ritualistic behavior in their own parallel reality. Students with ASD may not see the humor in a joke or when a typical person is being sarcastic. As an adult, they may remain without friends and isolated.

The main part of the brain that is affected by autism in the cerebellum. The cerebellum controls motor functions, speech/language development, and attention. Excessive neuron activity may be a cause of ASD characteristics. Sometimes, high performing students with ASD can realize these characteristics and make attempts to behave typically. They can suppress many of the characteristics and appear to manifest typical behavior. They overcome these challenges associated with autism, and control these traits, but will never be cured of ASD. Individuals with severe or profound ASD for the most part will not be able to control these traits and may require support for the rest of their lives.

Comorbid Disabilities/Disorders

There are several comorbid disabilities and disorders that are manifested by students who have ASD. The two most common are social skill deficits and speech/language disorders. Social skill deficits refer to an individual's inability to interact with other individuals. Students with this comorbidity find it challenging to make friends, enter group activities or conversations. They are loners many times and are hesitant to participate in class activities. Individuals with speech/language disorders manifest lack of pragmatic language skills, language fluency or appropriate language syntax, and understanding how to communicate intentions to join into an ongoing conversation of others. These individuals have problems fitting in. There is a correlation between social skill deficits and speech/language disorders because to develop social skills, speech/language must also develop. If an individual cannot converse, it will be challenging to develop socially. On the other hand, if an individual is not exposed to social situations and remain isolated, that person will not adequately develop language skills. In some cases, the individual will remain non-verbal throughout his or her lifetime.

Other comorbidities include ADHD, Echolalia, Emotional Disability (ED), Learning Disability (LD), Intellectual Disability (ID), sensory disorders, and motor skill disabilities. Later chapters will focus on these comorbidities. These disabilities and disorders can be manifested by individuals without ASD as well. Studies have indicated the brain of individuals with ASD show differences. An abnormal area of the brain of individuals with ASD include a reduced size in areas of cerebellum. The amygdala and hippocampus have a reduced size; however, the amygdala may hold more density. Lopes in the cerebrum are larger than normal. See Section I. of the Appendix for approximate locations in the brain. The ventricles are larger, and the caudate nucleus has less volume (Baron-Cohen and Belmonte, 2005).

Treatments

Treatments for ASD can start as early as a few months after birth and can continue well into adulthood of the individual. The key is to be diagnosed with ASD as early as possible after birth. Early diagnosis of ASD improves the individual's developmental outcomes because of earlier interventions (Page, Lustenberger, and Fröhlich, 2020). There are three main interventions used to treat individuals with ASD. Applied Behavior Analysis (ABA), Treatment and

Education of Autistic and Communication-Handicapped Children (TEACCH), and Behavioral Educational Intervention (BEI). Although, the results of these interventions were low to moderate, all students with ASD showed an improvement regardless of the intervention utilized (Mazza et al., 2020). Other treatments are related to the comorbidities associated with ASD. These include speech/language, social skills, and occupational therapies that are common in public and private schools. Teachers in a self-contained classroom environment can develop and apply ABA interventions. Teachers can solicit the help of the school psychologist and paraprofessional support to carry out these interventions.

Medications

In many cases, medications are given to students with ASD. There is no known medication for the treatment of ASD, but students are given medication for conditions related to Autism. These conditions are aggression, anxiety, and hyperactivity. The U.S. Food and Drug Administration (FDA) has approved the use of antipsychotic drugs, such as risperidone and aripripazole (Abilify), for treating irritability associated with ASD in children between certain ages (Mostafavi and Gaitanis, 2020). Other medications given for students with ASD are given for conditions related to comorbidities. Many of these medications control inappropriate and aggressive behaviors. Other medications are prescribed to control side effects of risperidone. See Section II. of the Appendix for List of Drugs with explanations of how they are used for treatment.

Teaching Students with ASD

Teaching students with ASD requires a lot of patience on the part of the educators. At times, the teacher is required to repeat the concepts 20 times or more. Explanation given must be in a very explicit and succinct language. Words spoken must be very simple and easy to understand. Having reading assignments that require inferencing or implicit language may not be very well understood by students with autism. Educators must apply scientific-based methods when teaching. Understand how different students learn best. Some students are visual learners and others are tactile learners. Check out different learning styles online and apply the strategies associated with each of these learning styles. Classroom assignments must be differentiated according to the cognitive level of the individual student. Every student is different and applying just one strategy may not work for all students. General education teachers should seek advice and work together with special education counterparts.

Conclusions

Educators must understand the complexities of this student disorder and how teaching strategies will hinder or enhance learning. It is important that educators know their students as well as their background, culture, and parents or caretakers. Having knowledge of the socio-economic level of the students is extremely important. Autism is a complex neurological disorder on a spectrum from very mild to severe and pervasive. Some students can become self-supporting adults and lead a very productive life. Others will require support for the rest of their lives. It is a good practice to have on-going communication with the parents and family of the student with ASD.

Recommendations

Educators should learn as much as possible about ASD and the different comorbid disabilities and disorders associated with autism. It is especially important that general educators become familiar with ASD as well because more students with ASD are becoming part of the inclusive classroom environment. More professional development and additional classes focusing on ASD and other student disorders is needed. An improved knowledge of evidence-based practices and knowing the students' needs will enhance the overall learning and progress of both typical and atypical students.

Chapter 3
Bipolar Disorder

Introduction

This chapter will focus on Bipolar Disorder. Bipolar disorder is a manic-depressive mental illness that usually develops during the teenage years and continues throughout life. It can be challenging to interact with individuals with bipolar disorder because of changes in their mood. One moment, these individuals are happy and the next moment, they are sad or aggressive. There are interventions and evidence-based practices are applied for controlling the condition. This disorder can hinder the academic progress and social skill development of adolescents in high school because of mood swings. Bipolar disorder can be treated, and individuals with this disorder can lead a fruitful and productive lives. Therapy is offered by mental health specialists, including psychiatrists, psychologists, and social workers. This chapter will explore comorbid disorders including social skills deficit, speech/language disorders, characteristics and traits, comorbid disorders, treatment, medications, and teaching students with bipolar disorder.

What is Bipolar Disorder?

Bipolar Disorder is a manic-depressive brain condition that causes irregular mood-shifts to occur. These changes in mood include energy and activity levels and hinders the ability to carry out daily life routines. These mood swings are different from common ups and downs that individuals normally have. Bipolar symptoms can hamper performance at school or on the job, strain relationships, and without treatment can lead to suicide (Bauer and Pfennig, 2005). According to the *Diagnostic and Statistical Manual of Mental Disorders* (DSM-5), there are four categories of bipolar disorders. These are

Bipolar-I, Bipolar-II, Bipolar Disorder Not Otherwise Specified (BP-NOS), and Cyclothymic Disorder (American Psychiatric Association, 2013). These categories will be described in the next section.

Characteristics/Traits

There are four main categories of bipolar disorders to consider. Bipolar-I has manic or mixed incidents are severe that may require urgent hospitalization. Manic incidents also occur and can last up to two weeks. Bipolar-II has a pattern of depressive incidents and hypomanic incidents. The incidents are not full-blown manic or mixed and may not require hospitalization. BP-NOS is diagnosed when characteristics of the disorder occur but do not meet diagnostic norms for either bipolar I or II. Lastly, Cyclothymic Disorder is when the individual has a mild form of bipolar disorder with manic-depressive mood cycles but does not meet the norms for any of the types of bipolar disorders.

Rapid cycling can occur when the mood of the individual changes from depression, mania, hypomania, or mixed states four or more times a year. Rapid cycling can occur with the individuals has the first incident at an earlier age. Bipolar disorder can affect both males and females of any race, ethnicity, and socioeconomic level. There are several comorbid disorders and disabilities to consider. Types of mania individuals experience are exaggerated optimism, aggressive behavior, increased irritability, decreased need for rest or sleep, grandiose thoughts, reckless behavior, and in more severe cases delusion and hallucination. Types of depression experienced is anxiety, sadness or crying, changes in appetite, worry, pessimism, loss of energy, feeling guilty, or in extreme cases thoughts of death or suicide.

Comorbid Disabilities/Disorders

Some comorbid illnesses include migraine headaches, obesity, type-II diabetes, thyroid illness, and cardiovascular diseases. Many studies consider ADHD, ODD, and Social Skills Deficit as comorbid disorders. According to a study of Goldstein et al. (2017) when diagnosing, it is essential not to count overlapping diagnostic symptoms of ADHD. This can lead to falsely indicated high rates of comorbidity. Bipolar disorder and high-functioning ASD are commonly comorbid and increasing evidence indicates that these comorbidities have a growing occurrence of suicidal mentation and behavior

(Masi et al., 2020). Areas of the brain the affect bipolar disorder development is the chemical flow into and through the gray matter in the frontal cortex, temporal, and parietal regions in both hemispheres. See Section I. of the Appendix for approximate locations in the brain. Flow of dopamine, noradrenaline, and serotonin to these areas of the brain may be impaired or underdeveloped (Buoli et al., 2017). This impaired flow affects the connectivity of the neurons.

Bipolar disorder is considered congenial and has no cure. There are treatments available to help control the mood swings prevalent in bipolar disorder. These treatments have been successful in allowing individuals with dipolar disorder to lead normal lifestyles and become self-supporting adults and have families. If this disorder is left untreated, the associated conditions will worsen over time.

Treatments

Psychotherapy is available. Cognitive behavioral and family-focused therapy will improve the symptoms associated with bipolar disorder. Cognitive Behavioral Therapy (CBT) refers to types of psychotherapy that treat mental health disorders. School psychologists, behavioralists, and counselors are responsible to helping students who have bipolar and other mental disorders as well. The purpose of CBT is to target inappropriate behaviors associated with the mental disorders. CBT functions on the premise that overt behaviors are learned and through therapy these behaviors can be changed or replaced.

Family focused therapy involves giving the family the information and necessary tools to help the family member with bipolar disorder. Families work together with a family mental health therapist to help improve the relationship and interaction with the parents, siblings, other family members, and the individual with bipolar disorder. This therapy has proven successful and gives family members new support roles in dealing with this mental disorder. Another alternative to controlling bipolar disorder is through drugs.

Medications

Several medications are prescribed to control bipolar disorder. A mental healthcare expert will determine what type of medication is best for the individual with bipolar disorder. How individuals respond to the medication is different and various. Mood stabilizers are the most typical medication to be prescribed for bipolar disorder. These drugs include Lithium, Depakote, Valproic Acid, Tegretol, Equetro, Quetiapine, and Lamictal. These drugs, like most others have side effects that varies from person to person. See Section II. of the Appendix for List of Drugs with explanations of how they are used for treatment.

Frequently, combined therapeutic and pharmaceutical approaches to treating bipolar disorders have met with considerable success. According to a study of Swartz et al. (2018), the outcome of this quantitative study was significant. Participants with bipolar disorder attended 45-minute therapy sessions; they were also given Quetiapine, an atypical antipsychotic drug and Placebo, a fake pill. After 20 weeks of therapy, there was noted improvement in the mood shifts of the participants.

Teaching Students with Bipolar Disorder

Teaching students with bipolar disorder requires a lot of educator preparation, awareness of bipolar disorder, and patience. There should be accommodations in place. Students will benefit from more time to complete assignments. Educators must give succinct and clear explanations and instructions. Students must have the opportunities to ask for clarifications if needed. Assignments must be broken down. Classroom interventions are also important. There must be less distractions. Distractions can trigger a bipolar mood swing. Outline and visuals are useful to help students better understand the class assignment or concept. Behavior management is extremely important. To avoid inappropriate behavior, assignments must be organized and delivered with flexibility. Educators must be aware when the student is manifesting signs of fatigue, anxiety, or agitation. These signs can trigger a mood swing. Following these simple procedures can enhance the academic and behavioral progress of the student. Evidence-based practices like UDL and UbD will solidify the success of both the educator and the student.

Conclusions

Bipolar Disorder is a lifelong condition, but it can be managed with therapy and medication so that the person with this disorder can lead a fulfilling life. Educators must be aware of the different traits of bipolar disorder. Some different comorbid disorders exhibit characteristics like bipolar disorder. Many of the medications used to control this disorder are also prescribed for other medical and mental disorders as well. Behaviors exhibited by students who have some disorders can trigger mood swings in bipolar disorder. Behavioral meltdowns triggered by a classroom event can become worse if the meltdown is exacerbated by another disorder. Classroom interventions must target what different events trigger the behavioral meltdown before it occurs. Educators must be prepared to de-escalate behaviors that cause meltdowns.

Recommendations

Educators must be ready to deal with bipolar behavior. In addition, they must also understand other mental disorders that are comorbid with bipolar disorder. More time must be spent learning about mental disorders in teacher certification courses to better prepare future educators. Reading IEPs Iof special-needs students will help those interacting with these students be in a better position to use the appropriate strategy or intervention that works best with the student. Being unaware of the appropriate evidence-based practices or not using evidence-based practices at all may cause some students to exhibit violent physical and verbal behaviors that may put everyone in the classroom in an unsafe situation.

Chapter 4
Echolalia

Introduction

This chapter will focus on Echolalia. Students with echolalia are in many general education classrooms. Echolalia is a verbal disorder that many educators have limited knowledge of. Educators can become frustrated with a student who repeats whatever is asked or stated. Echolalia is comorbid with a variety of neurological and psychiatric disorders, especially ASD. Many novice educators believe the student is trying to make fun of them. They fail to understand why this behavior occurs and what is responsible for the student's delay in answering the question or elaborating. This chapter will cover characteristics, comorbid disabilities and disorders, treatments, medications, and teaching students with Echolalia.

What is Echolalia?

Echolalia a congenial disorder characterized by pointless repetition of another person's spoken words as a symptom of this psychiatric disorder (Stiegler, 2015). Students with echolalia may only be able to repeat a teacher's question rather than answer it. Students with echolalia are trying to communicate the answer, learn spoken language or practice it.

There is a difference between Echolalia and Tourette Syndrome. Tourette syndrome is when a student may unexpectedly yell or say random things as part of their tic. The student has no control over what is said or when it is said. Echolalia is when a student will repeat only after what was said (Grossi et al., 2013). In the case of a student with autism when trying to communicate, there is lack of inhibitory control so the question will be repeated rather than being answered. Inhibitory control is an executive brain cognitive process function.

Studies focusing on best practices for students with echolalia is limited. Due to contrasting descriptions of echolalia within research, inconsistent and limited assessment methods, and other behavioral approaches with different viewpoints, professionals are faced with a challenge to provide comprehensive evidence-based interventions (Stiegler, 2015).

Characteristics/Traits

Students with echolalia repeat sounds and expressions that they hear. They are challenged with being able to communicate successfully because they have trouble conveying their own thoughts. For example, a student with echolalia might only be able to repeat a question rather than answer it. The repetitive speech patterns characteristic to echolalia have been described in different ways. Literature focuses on two types of echolalia; immediate and delayed. Immediate echolalia refers to phrases or speech patterns repeated after it is heard. Delayed echolalia refers to a student using phrases or speech out of context. For example, a teacher always played a game during "free time" in the classroom. The student utters "free time" instead of the name of the game (van Santen et al., 2013). Students repeat what they hear to give them more time to process the question that was asked.

Comorbid Disabilities/Disorders

Some other disabilities and disorder simultaneously occurring with echolalia are ASD, Schizophrenia, and Dysphonia. Causes of echolalia are related to Transcortical Sensory Aphasia, degenerative brain diseases, and head traumas. Transcortical Sensory Aphasia (TSA) may be produced by a lesion in the inferior left temporal lobe of the brain near Wernicke's area. See Section I. of the Appendix for approximate locations in the brain. A characteristic of TSA is impaired auditory comprehension and may impact fluent speech and repetition (Boatman et al., 2000). Echolalia can be caused by head traumas as well.

Treatments

Echolalia is treated with speech therapy, medications, and home care. Echolalia as a maladaptive form of speech is often viewed as a behavior. Therefore, Applied Behavior Analysis (ABA) as an evidence-based practice is used to target echolalia (Stiegler, 2015). Many educators misinterpret the student repetition of the question or statement as being a sign of disrespect. According to his study, there are different approaches to target echolalia. Differential reinforcement of other behaviors, matched stimulation, redirection, and response interruption were ABA approaches mentioned.

Medications

Echolalia can be treated with antidepressants or anxiety medications to mitigate the side effects of this disorder. These medications do not treat the condition itself but using medication will help the individual stay calm. Echolalia can be exacerbated when a person is upset or has anxiety. Medications utilized are serotonin reuptake inhibitors (SRIs) that work by increasing the levels of the neurotransmitter serotonin in the brain and include fluoxetine (Prozac) and citalopram (Celexa). For a student with echolalia and ASD, these medications do not effectively alleviate flapping manifested in students with ASD (Reddihough, 2019; Herscu et al., 2019; King, 2009). See Section II. of the Appendix for List of Drugs with explanations of how they are used for treatment.

Teaching Students with Echolalia

In addition to speech/language therapy sessions that should be provided to students with echolalia, there are some evidence-based teaching strategies that will benefit students with echolalia. Keep in mind that students with echolalia usually have ASD as well. When students are repeating the questions that are asked, they are trying to communicate answers. This is a processing delay in the brain that hinders their ability to answer. Some students with echolalia can use writing to convey their answers.

Instead of using language to communicate, use writing. Paper and pencils are an extension of what you express verbally. Make sure you engage the students and base the writing level on their appropriate cognitive level. This strategy is good for enhancing social interaction as well. Written communication gives students the opportunity to go back and repeat what was written. This helps to clarify what thought is being conveyed. Script training with visual cues is another intervention used to help students with echolalia (Charlop-Christy and Kelso, 2003).

The use of sentence stems is another strategy to use in the classroom. Instead of asking the student "What do you want?" prompt the student by stating "I want to _____" and wait for an answer. One word can be used to identify what you want, like "science." You can adjust your sentence stem to reflect what you are teaching. This procedure takes a lot of time but acts as an assurance that the student has enough language development to respond (Perkins, 1994).

Lastly, computer-based interventions are used with students with ASD and echolalia. Computer-based interventions enhances language development of these students. A software program was developed for everyday living skills in the areas of food, hygiene, and play. According to Hetzroni and Tannous (2004), results of their study indicated that the students produced fewer sentences with delayed and irrelevant speech.

Conclusions

Echolalia is a congenial disorder characterized by the repetition of spoken words. Students with Echolalia are challenged in conveying their thoughts. Principle comorbidities occurring with Echolalia include ASD, Schizophrenia, and speech/language disorders such as Dysphonia. Causes of echolalia are neurological and genetic but can be brought about by traumatic head injuries. Treatments for echolalia are speech/language therapy, ABA, homecare, and medication.

Teaching students with echolalia utilize evidence-based practices as well as computer-based interventions. These practices can be the same as those implemented for students with ASD. Autism is a very common comorbidity alongside echolalia. Educators, therapists, and psychologists who interact with such students must be patient. One slight miscommunication or misunderstanding can trigger a student's melt-down in a classroom or therapy setting. Try to keep the student calm. Educators must give the student time to answer the question. The student may repeat the question and stop. Try asking the question a different way. Eventually, the student may be able to answer.

Recommendations

Because echolalia is not well understood and only superficially covered in teacher training and certification courses, educators should learn as much as possible about this disorder in order improve classroom management and learning expectations of students. Research is uncovering cutting edge evidence-based practices that can control behavior of students with ASD and echolalia. Better prepared educators lead to improved implementation of these practices. This preparedness has revealed improved communication with students and enhanced learning occurring.

Chapter 5
Emotional Disability

Introduction

ED is a psychopathological disorder that manifests calamity associated with emotional and mental illnesses. Individuals with ED lose excessive days from school and work, reduced feelings of well-being, and require professional mental healthcare intervention. Because of ED, these individuals are challenged performing day-to-day activities. This is a major concern voiced by these individuals and their families (Kouzis and Eaton, 1994). The scope of this chapter is to be able to identify and understand ED, its characteristics, comorbidities, treatments, teaching evidence-based practices. Knowledge of these factors will lead to a better educational outcome. This outcome will enhance pedagogical instances showing students and teachers working and learning together.

What is Emotional Disability (ED)?

An Emotional disability is a condition that adversely affects a student's educational progress over a period. The inability to learn is triggered by emotional factors that cannot be described by cognitive, sensory, or health factors (Kouzis and Eaton, 1994). Six of the main emotional disorders include anxiety disorders, bipolar disorder, conduct disorders, eating disorders, obsessive-compulsive disorder (OCD) and psychotic disorders (Gottfried and Harven, 2014). The outcomes of anxiety, fear or other emotional-based conditions can be the causation of maladaptive behaviors including withdrawal, isolation, and anger and aggression. These behaviors unfavorably affect a student's academic and social standing (American Psychiatric

Association, 2020). Federal and state regulations state an emotional disability as unsuitable types of behavior or feelings under normal conditions.

Characteristics/Traits

Aggression, hyperactivity, and withdrawal are the main characteristics of ED. Aggression may include violent and self-injurious behavior and fighting. Hyperactivity can relate to short attention span and impulsiveness. Lastly, withdrawal is when students do not interact with others socially. Students may also exhibit excessive fear or anxiety. Other traits exhibited are bipolar disorders, eating disorders, obsessive-compulsive disorder (OCD) and psychotic disorders. These disorders can be very disruptive in school classrooms. Individuals with ED are excessively absent from their school and work settings, do not feel good about themselves, and require specialized mental healthcare intervention. Because of ED, these individuals are challenged performing day-to-day activities. The inability to learn can be triggered by both environmental, genetic factors or comorbid disorders.

Comorbid Disabilities/Disorders

Comorbidities include ADHD, ASD, ODD, hypertension, heart disease, seizures, speech/language deficits, social disorders, energy, fatigue, and cancer. The presence of these comorbidities varies among different students. Some students may experience one or more of these conditions, and others may not experience any of these conditions. The comorbidities manifested may be non-existent, mild, moderate, and/or severe. The primary region of the brain associated with emotional disorders is the amygdala. The amygdala processes emotional events. See Section I. of the Appendix for approximate location in the brain.

Treatments

ED are usually treated in combination with cognitive-behavioral therapy, social skill therapy, group psychotherapy, relaxation techniques, or medications. Cognitive behavioral therapy (CBT) is a psychological intervention that has been shown effective when utilized to treat alcohol and drug-use challenges, anxiety disorders, depression, eating disorders, marital problems, and severe mental illness. Numerous studies indicate that improvement of emotional disorders occurred after CBT was implemented more so than when other forms of psychological interventions or psychotic medications (American Psychological Association, 2021). CBT intervention focuses on defective or unaccommodating ways of thinking. Learned patterns of inappropriate behavior and modifying thinking patterns.

Family psychoeducation provides immediate family members therapy designed to improve communication and resolve conflicts. This therapy is usually provided by a clinical social worker or psychologist. Social skill therapy is provided by trained school social workers in school settings. Group psychotherapy involves one or more psychologists or therapists who lead a group of two or more students with ED. Groups meet for an hour or two every week. Therapy sessions will vary among different individuals. Relaxation techniques is a way to combat stress involving deep breathing, meditation, or yoga. In many cases, medications are used to help alleviate ED.

Medications

Medications prescribed for ED include Norpramin (desipramine) and Tofranil (imipramine) for treatment of anxiety, depression, and obsessive and compulsive behavior associated with anxiety disorders, depression, ADHD, OCD, autism
, and Tourette syndrome. These same medications are prescribed to treat other disorders mentioned in this book. Antihistamines, benzodiazepines, and a medicine called Buspirone are prescribed to control anxiety. These drugs affect body chemicals to act directly in certain parts of the brain to help alleviate feeling of anxiety.

Teaching Students with ED

More and more students with ED are receiving some or all their instruction in inclusive classroom setting. General and special educators must be equipped to address both diverse academic and non-academic needs of students with ED using evidence-based practices. The teaching strategies that have proven effective include keeping class rules and activities succinct and explicit, permit minibreaks during class, treat all students fair, and use strategies to motivate the students to learn (Gable et al., 2012). Experienced and well-trained educators are the most important part of effective programs for students with ED.

Conclusions

Emotional Disability (ED) is a condition that adversely affects a student's educational progress over a period. The outcomes of anxiety, fear, or other emotional-based conditions can be the causation of maladaptive behaviors including withdrawal, isolation, and anger and aggression. Aggression, hyperactivity, and withdrawal are the main characteristics of ED. Comorbidities include ADHD, ASD, ODD, hypertension, heart disease, seizures, speech/language deficits, social disorders, energy, fatigue, and cancer. ED are usually treated in combination with cognitive-behavioral therapy, social skill therapy, group psychotherapy, relaxation techniques, or medications. Medications prescribed for ED include Norpramin (desipramine) and Tofranil (imipramine) for treatment of anxiety, depression, and obsessive and compulsive behavior. General and special educators must be equipped to address both diverse academic and non-academic needs of students with ED using evidence-based practices.

Recommendations

Many novice educators and seasoned general educators have knowledge of evidence-based practices; however, they do not possess sufficient understanding of how to apply these theory-based practices. Because more of students with ED and other disabilities are now in inclusive classroom settings, more hands-on training through professional development in the classroom is needed to help close the gap of lack of experience in applying evidence-based practices. There should be more teacher certification courses dedicated to understanding how to apply evidence-based practices in all classroom settings. Educators must be patient when teaching students with ED.

Chapter 6
Fetal Alcohol Syndrome Disorder

Introduction

Fetal Alcohol Syndrome (FASD) is responsible for the causes of other developmental disabilities mentioned in this book. FASD is a prevalent syndrome manifested in students when their biological mothers indulged in the excessive use of alcohol during pregnancy. Drinking alcohol during pregnancy can cause a woman's baby to be born with birth defects and developmental disabilities. Beer, wine, or hard liquor are the leading causes of preventable birth defects and developmental disabilities in the United States. This chapter focuses on what FASD curtains, characteristics and traits manifested, comorbidities, treatments, medications, and teaching students with FASD.

What is Fetal Alcohol Syndrome (FASD)?

FASD is a condition in a student that result from excessive use of alcohol, medications, and illegal substances by their biological mother during pregnancy. FASD is responsible for brain damage and growth difficulties. There is no amount of alcohol that is considered safe. The conditions of FASD vary from student to student, but the defects cannot be reversed (Mayo Clinic, 2021). Students with FASD have irregular arms, legs, fingers, and joints. There is slow growth before and after birth. Some students may experience challenges with their vision and hearing. They may have a smaller head circumference and brain size and experience heart defects and complications with development of bones and kidneys. FASD can be prevented. Women who are pregnant should not drink alcoholic beverages, take medications without their physician's approval, and never use illegal drugs. It has not been determined what amount of alcohol is considered safe to use during pregnancy.

Characteristics/Traits

Distinctive facial features, including small eyes, an exceptionally thin upper lip, a short, upturned nose, and a smooth skin surface between the nose and upper lip are visible characteristics of individuals with FASD. Students may exhibit problems with the brain and central nervous system including deficits in coordination and balance, poor memory, reasoning and problem-solving challenges, and challenges identifying consequences of choices. Many students with FASD may experience eating disorders and encopresis or urinary incontinence.

Comorbid Disabilities/Disorders

There are many comorbidities associated with FASD. These include: Intellectual Disability (IT), Learning Disorders (LD), delayed development, challenges with paying attention, challenges staying on task, jitteriness, hyperactivity (ADHD), rapidly changing moods, bipolar disorders, behavior, or impulse control (ODD), poor judgment of time, trouble adapting to change or switching from one task to another, getting along with others, social skill deficits, and ASD. These students have difficulty in a classroom setting (Mayo Clinic, 2021). Usually, an individual with FAS has a smaller brain than normal. The part that are affected by FAS is the basal ganglia, cerebellum, corpus callosum, and the hippocampus. See Section I. of the Appendix for approximate locations in the brain. The normal development of these parts of the brain is disrupted due to exposure to alcohol. This condition is caused when a mother indulges in alcoholic beverage while pregnant.

Treatments

Presently, there is no cure or detailed treatment for FASD. Physical defects and mental deficits usually last for one's entire life. There are early intervention services that may reduce the effects of FASD and can prevent some secondary disabilities. The intervention team includes a special and general educator, school psychologist, speech-language, occupation, and physical therapists. These individuals make part of the student's individualized education plan (IEP) and multi-disciplinary evaluation team (MET). Early interventions will help with fine and gross motor skills, speech-language, and social skill deficits. The in-school team may determine support services to help with learning and behavioral challenges. Students with FASD may be given medications to help with comorbidities of this disorder.

Medications

Due to the factor that FASD has no cure, there are no approved medications available currently. However, there are medications available to treat some of the comorbid and secondary disorders and disabilities of FASD. These include Norpramin (desipramine) and Tofranil (imipramine) for treatment of anxiety, depression, and obsessive and compulsive behavior associated with anxiety disorders, depression, ADHD, OCD, autism, and Tourette syndrome. Antihistamines, benzodiazepines, and a medicine called Buspirone are prescribed to control anxiety. See Section II of the Appendix for List of Drugs with explanations of how they are used for treatment.

Teaching Students with FASD

Teaching methods and strategies for students with FASD may be the same as some the other disabilities and disorders mentioned in this book. The classroom setting must be structured, steady, have an unchanging routine, explanations must be succinct and to the point, and have constant repetition. Educators must be patient and education team must be in constant contact with parents and/or caretakers to discuss continuity of methods and strategies for the student at home. Evidence-based practices should be used when teaching students with FASD because these practices have a high success rate when instructing and applying behavioral strategies in the classroom.

Conclusions

And FASD is responsible for the cause of many other developmental disabilities. It is a prevalent syndrome manifested by students whose biological mothers indulged in the use of alcoholic beverages, excessive use of medications, and the use of illegal drugs. Distinctive facial features are prevalent with individuals with this disorder. There is no cure or detailed treatment for FASD, but early diagnosis and therapy will improve behavioral constraints associated with this disorder. Educators must utilize evidence-based practices in the classroom. On-going professional development will enhance professional awareness of this mental disorder. Continuous professional development and training is important because practices are constantly changing and what is perceived to be an acceptable classroom practice may no longer be acceptable as years pass.

Recommendations

It is highly recommended that educators are familiar with FASD to ameliorate their interactions with students with FASD. Parents should be made aware of the dangers of alcohol and illegal drug consumption during pregnancy because there is no cure for FASD as the effects cannot be reversed. There should be more emphasis placed on understanding FASD in courses during the teaching certification process. Professional development by both novice and seasoned educators should be continuous and ongoing.

Chapter 7
Hyperosmia

Introduction

The chapter focuses on Hyperosmia. Hyperosmia is a sensory disorder that is the cause of an increased olfactory acuity (Del Casale, 2020). This is an increased sense of smell induced by sensitivity to chemicals. Hyperosmia is a medically neuro-genetic unexplained condition. There are many characteristics associated with hyperosmia with comorbidities correlated to other disabilities and disorders. There are treatments available for relief of the symptoms but there is no cure for hyperosmia. Teaching students with Hyperosmia in the classroom can be challenging because of their heightened sense of smell that can be annoying causing classroom disruption to occur.

What is Hyperosmia?

Hyperosmia is an increased sense of smell induced by sensitivity to chemicals. Causes of this disorder is genetic but environmental constraints can also be a factor. Other neurological conditions that may cause hyperosmia include epilepsy, pulps or tumors in the nose or brain, and multiple sclerosis. Head injuries, allergies, and dental problems can cause hyperosmia.

This sensory disorder occurs when odor molecules enter the nasal cavity and contact olfactory receptors. This causes an abnormally increased signal at any point between the olfactory receptors and the olfactory sensory nerve. Students with hyperosmia will manifest a lot of discomfort and in some cases illnesses from certain smells. When exposed to odors, toxic exhausts, and gas, the discomforts associated with hyperosmia will be exacerbated and can lead to anxiety and depression. Perfumes, synthetic fragrances, and cleaning products can also trigger discomfort. The discomforts experienced from odors will vary from one individual to the next.

Characteristics/Traits

Some characteristics of hyperosmia are itchy, plugged up or runny nose, shortness of breath, coughing, headaches, wheezing, false sense of smelling, itchy throat, and redness of the eyes. Other factors that contribute to hyperosmia can be personal,, and environmental constraints (Fard et al., 2018). Students will not exhibit all these characteristics the same; however, headaches are the most prevalent of these traits. Air pollution inside classrooms caused by dirty or contaminated air conditioning vents, and airborne pathogens are responsible for causing or exacerbating existing cases of hyperosmia. An opposite effect that some students exhibit is lack of smell.

Comorbid Disabilities/Disorders

According to the study of Han et al. (2020), ASD is a genetic disorder that has a high comorbidity with hyperosmia. Students with autism have a greater susceptibility to auditory, visual, or tactile stimuli disorders. Other comorbidities include psychosocial disorder, emotional disorder (ED), depression and anxiety, ADHD, and bipolar disorder. Students with autism and hyperosmia can become disruptive in the classroom due to the discomfort experienced by an over-stimulus of a certain smell or scent. This condition can greatly influence the academic progress and behavior of this group of students. Educators must have interventions in place to help these students cope with this condition.

The part of the brain that is subjected to hyperosmia is the amygdala. This is the region of the brain that processes emotion. The hippocampus is another part affected by hyperosmia. This region regulates cognition and memory. The smell enters the nose through olfactory bulb that runs directly to the base of the brain connecting to the amygdala. See Section I. of the Appendix for approximate locations in the brain.

Treatments

There is no effective cure or therapy available for hyperosmia; however, temporary relief from conditions of hyperosmia includes chewing a menthol-flavored gum, like peppermint, or sucking on strong eucalyptus lozenges. Students should be allowed to move away from the smell stimulus causing their discomfort. Treatments using medication exist and can relieve discomforts of hyperosmia and keep the occurrences of classroom disruption at a minimum. In some individuals with hyperosmia, abnormal growth of a polyp or tumor can provoke altered sensitivity to certain smells. Undergoing surgery to remove these growths may alleviate the sensory sensitivity. Avoiding smells that trigger the over sensitivity may also help. Avoiding foods with strong smells can also mitigate the symptom of hyperosmia. Hypnosis and self-hypnosis have been used to treat many individuals across the United States. Individuals can be hypnotically trained to control their senses. Hypnosis may not work in all cases.

Medications

There are several medications that can be prescribed to relieve discomforts related to hyperosmia. These include oxymetazoline spray as a decongestant and anesthetic sprays to numb your olfactory nerve cells and can be used alone or with other drugs to treat hyperosmia. See Section II. of the Appendix for List of Drugs with explanations of how they are used for treatment. Students and their family should consult with an otolaryngologist (throat, nose, and ear physician) or mental health professional in the case of students with another developmental or psychological disorders.

Teaching Students with Hyperosmia

In most cases, educators will be teaching students with other developmental disorders such as ASD with hyperosmia as a comorbid disorder. To keep students from being triggered by scents and strong odors, it is important to keep the classroom free from these smells. This includes perfumes, colognes, and cleaning materials or anything else that has a strong odor. Evidence based practices used in the classroom should apply to what is best for the disorder or disability of the student present in the classroom. Like most disabilities and disorders, educators must exercise patience, be explicit and succinct when explaining or modeling a new academic concept. There are few therapies for hyperosmia in the classroom. Most students with hyperosmia rely on medication for relieve from the over stimulus of their sense of smell.

Conclusions

Hyperosmia is a sensory disorder that causes an over-stimulus of one's sense of smell that has no known cure. Common comorbid disabilities include ASD, ADHD, bipolar disorder, anxiety, ED/LD, and behavior challenges. There are few therapies that exist for this disorder, but medications are prescribed to help control the over-stimulus associated with smell. Educators must rely on evidence-based practices relative to the comorbidities of the other disorders and disabilities associated with hyperosmia.

Recommendations

Educators should become familiar with hyperosmia and its comorbidities. Over time, experience is the best teacher, but professional development and training will better prepare the novice educator for the classroom. If educators can understand and apply what was learned during their teacher certification courses, they will be more successful with classroom management and the academic progress of their students. Special and general educators must be better prepared to confront the challenges these disabilities and disorders present.

Chapter 8
Intellectual Disability (ID)

Introduction

Intellectual Disability (ID) is a leading cause for lack of progress of students in school classrooms across the United States. Students with ID have difficulty while thinking and trying to understand. Three of the most common causes of ID include Fetal Alcohol Syndrome, Downs Syndrome, and Fragile X Syndrome. There are many characteristics of ID that are like ASD and LD. This chapter will focus on what ID is, its characteristics and traits and distinguish them from comorbidities. Treatments and medication used with students will be explored. Teaching students with ID can be challenging for educators but, applying the right evidenced-based practices in the classroom can enhance the progress of this population of students.

What is an Intellectual Disability (ID)?

Intellectual Disability is defined as limited abilities to learn, to solve problems, socialize, converse, and communicate, and function in day-to-day life. Three main areas of deficits prevalent in ID are conceptual, which include language, reading, writing, math, reasoning, and memory. Social skills may be affected that include the ability to empathize, make judgment, affectingly communicate with others, and the ability to follow rules and have friends. Practical areas include everyday living skills, being responsible (job and school), money management, and organization (Parekh, 2017). Students with ID have a below average IQ and are challenged with making judgments and have behavioral problems. An average IQ is between 85 and 115. ID is caused by genetic disorders and can be passed down from parents. ID cannot be reversed and is not curable. Intellectual disability is genetic but can also be caused by traumatic brain injury (TBI) because of accident from a fall, automobile accident, or intense blow to the head.

Characteristics/Traits

Characteristics of ID include gross and fine motor skill deficits, sensory disorders, speech-language disorders, and challenges with cognitive skills. Because the characteristics of ID and learning disabilities (LD) are similar, these terms are used interchangeably. It is important to appropriately compare intellectual disabilities, and learning disorders (Angelka and Goran, 2018). Students with ID can manifest the same symptoms as students with LD; however, students without ID can manifest symptoms of LD. LD can occur in students within a sociocultural environment that does not encourage learning. Students can exhibit LD when parents do not motivate their children to learn or are unable to help. ID can occur at birth in many individuals and LD can be acquired during individual development or because of ID (Schalock et al., 2018). Students who have ID and LD can lead to their lack of progress and ultimate school failures without early and appropriate intervention (Angelka and Goran, 2018).

Comorbid Disabilities/Disorders

Comorbid disabilities and disorders include ADHD, ASD, Cerebral Palsy, Speech/Language, depression, anxiety disorders, and LD. Many times, autism can be overlooked in individuals who have been diagnosed with Intellectual Disability (ID) (Kiani et al., 2019). Congenital blindness is reported as a comorbid condition with intellectual disability; however, it has been discovered that congenital blindness is related to individuals diagnosed with Autism Spectrum Disorder (ASD). The main regions of the brain that affects ID is the occipital lobe and the temporal lobe. There is a cortical thinning in these regions of the brain that may be the cause of ID. See Section I. of the Appendix for approximate locations in the brain.

Treatments

ID is a lifelong condition; however, early diagnosis and ongoing therapy are recommended as an avenue to support students with ID. Ongoing intervention may improve functionalities of the student and help the student to succeed during their lifetime. Therapies used to treat ID are applied behavior analysis used by educators to encourage positive behavior, behavior therapy used to replace or modify inappropriate behavior, animal assisted therapy, developmental social pragmatic therapy, and sensory processing analysis. Dogs and other animals have proven successful. Most children like to be around animals and bond easily to them. It is important to note that the type of intervention and therapy used may be influenced by underlying medical or genetic conditions and comorbidities. In moderate and severe cases of ID, the use of drugs may be an alternative to therapy, especially when the condition causes inappropriate student behavior to be exhibited. In many cases, both therapy and the use of psychotropic drugs are used together.

Medications

Psychotropic drugs are also prescribed by psychiatrists and in some cases clinical psychologiststo control and alleviate ID. The main categories of psychotropic drugs are anti-anxiety medication, antidepressants, antipsychotics, mood stabilizers, and stimulants. These include Ativan, Celexa, Desyrel, Lexapro, Prozac, Xanax, and Zoloft. See Section II. of the Appendix for List of Drugs with explanations of how they are used for treatment. There is no cure or reversal treatment available for ID. It is a lifetime condition. Many of these drugs are prescribed to control behavioral conditions and comorbid disorders associated with ID.

Teaching Students with ID

Educators, therapists, school psychologists, and support staff may be challenged working with students with ID. Classroom evidence-based practices include differentiated lesson plans, use of student's multiple intelligences, strengths, and weaknesses of students with intellectual disabilities, use of manipulatives, and lesson modifications. These practices have proven successful when implementing components of UDL framework in inclusive classroom settings for students of intellectual disabilities. When interacting with students with ID, there should be efforts made to never call them kids, especially high-school-aged adolescents, and to use explicit, succinct, and simplified language. Speak slower to these students and do not shout at them or speak louder. Set classroom goals and expectations. Interact with them in a way that you would interact with a peer, but at the same time draw boundaries. Continuously ask them how they feel about a decision or practice used and ask them if they have any suggestions. Permit them to voice their opinions. Educators should use UDL, UBD, or another classroom practices that works best for them. Educators should also work closely with therapists, school psychologists, support staff, and parent/caregivers to have continuity of practices used in the classroom, during therapy, and at home. Working together will mitigate changes between the school and home environments.

Conclusions

Intellectual Disability (ID) is a lifetime non-curable condition that is defined as having limited abilities to learn, to solve problems, socialize, converse, and communicate, and function in day-to-day life. Characteristics of ID include gross and fine motor skill deficits, sensory disorders, speech-language disorders, and challenges with cognitive skills. Comorbid disabilities and disorders include ADHD, ASD, cerebral palsy, speech/language disorder, depression, anxiety disorders, and LD. Treatments for ID can involve psychotherapy, psychotropic medicine, or both. Educators should use evidence-based practices in the classroom that extends into the home of the student.

Recommendations

As more and more students with ID and other disabilities spend more of their school day in inclusive classroom setting, it is imperative that educators become familiar with ID and comorbidities associated with ID. Working directly with special educators, school psychologists, therapists, and other support staff will enhance classroom management and decrease appropriate behavior manifested in the classroom. Ongoing professional development and training will better prepare educators in confronting challenges associated with teaching students with ID.

Chapter 9
Learning Disability

Introduction

Learning Disability (LD) causes many students to underperform in school classroom. LD can occur because of genetic factors, trauma, and environmental factors. Children can be born with the disorder and inherit it from their families. LD can occur after traumatic accidents like a head injury and serious accidents due to a fall or automobile collision. Environmental factors are present when children are deprived of items common in middle-class households such as exposure to books, television, internet, friends, and parents who can converse, teach, and help their children learn. Many times, these children come from families who are part of lower socio-economic groups.

What is Learning Disability (LD)?

Individuals with challenges in specific cognitive development and academic progress with otherwise typical levels of intellectual functioning are considered as having a learning disability (LD) (Büttner and Hasselhorn, 2011). Students who have LD are common within communities where reading, writing, and math skills are required to function in everyday life. It is difficult to analyze and identify the causes of LD because it is unknown how cognitive disfunctions are related to learning disabilities (Landerl, Fussenegger, Moll, and Willburger, 2009). Learning disabilities will hinder the ability to learn job skills, development of social skills, and function as self-supporting adults. Early diagnosis of LD and intervention practices for students will improve their academic progress and living skills improvement.

Characteristics/Traits

Some characteristics of students manifest with LD include short attention span, poor memory, difficulty following directions, inability to discriminate between letters, numbers, and sounds, lack of phonological awareness, poor spelling skills, lack of number sense, and processing deficits. Processing deficits are challenges students encounter when attempting to recognize and interpret information taken in through the senses. Primarily, students may not be able to process what the hear or see. Students with poor processing of what they hear and see may not be able to stay focused in the classroom, they will exhibit poor memory skills, and will not be able to follow instructions because of lack of understanding. Students will be challenged in learning how to read due to lack of phonological awareness and the ability to distinguish between letters and numbers. Their writing skills will be influenced by poor spelling skills and fine motor skill deficits. They will have poor penmanship.

Comorbid Disabilities/Disorders

Comorbidities of LD include ADHD, ASD, Dyslexia (challenges with reading, writing, and spelling), Dyscalculia (lack of mathematical number sense and calculation skills), Written Expression Disorder, social skills development, speech/language deficits, gross and fine motor skills. Gross motors skills involve normal manner of walking, coordination of arms and legs, especially in sports. Fine motors skills involve being able to hold a pen, use tools involving the fingers and hands, and penmanship skills. Therapy is provided for learning disabilities and comorbidities. A Learning Disorder is caused by malfunctioning regions of the brain that include perisylvian and Wernicke's areas in the left back part of the temporal lobe and the Broca's region in the premotor section of the frontal lobe. See Section I of the Appendix for approximate locations in the brain.

Treatments

Treatment is available through speech/language pathologist, school social working, occupational therapists, behavioralists, and psychologists. The earlier the treatment is initiated, the better position the student will be in to learn a trade, go to college, and become a self-supporting adult. Treatment is available once the student is placed in an exceptional education program available in both public and private schools. Once multi-disciplinary evaluation team (MET) has determined eligibility for services under exceptional education, an individualized education plan (IEP) is developed. The educational team will determine what type of treatments and therapy will be available to the student.

Special accommodations may be required to be developed for the student. These accommodations include more time to turn in class assignments, modified classwork according to cognitive level of the student, and behavior intervention plans (BIP). Working with students in small groups or with focused paraprofessional support has proven successful with many students. Students who are cognitively challenged may require instructions or how to complete the classwork assignment repeated multiple times. In some cases, medication may be required to treat the condition(s) associated with LD. These medications are prescribed to control stress, anxiety, and attention deficits (Mayo Clinic, 2021).

Medications

Drugs prescribed for LD and comorbid disorders include Adderall, Ritalin, Metadate, and Vyvanse. See Section II of the Appendix for List of Drugs with explanations of how they are used for treatment. These drugs are prescribed for many of the comorbidities of LD such as ADHD. The medications contain amphetamines, dextroamphetamine, and stimulants that are used to control the body's impulse control and hyperactivity. The use of these medications may slow weight gain and body growth. Side effects noted are behavioral problems, lightheadedness, hallucinations, muscle twitches, vision changes, seizures.

Teaching Students with LD

Teaching students with LD can be overwhelming and challenging for educators. Having knowledge of the different students, their background, and disorders go a long way in reducing disruption and improving academic progress and social skill growth of these students. Many students with LD require one-on-one support. For them to grasp the concept or learn the steps, educators must be able to repeat what is being taught many times for the students to learn. Educators must be aware of the student's learning style. Many students are visual learners, but often they may learn using another learning style or combination of one or more styles. The seven learning styles include aural, visual, kinesthetic, verbal, logical, intrapersonal, and social. These learning styles can be used with other disabilities and disorders as well.

Conclusions

Individuals with challenges in specific cognitive development and academic progress with otherwise typical levels of intellectual functioning are considered as having a learning disability (LD) (Büttner and Hasselhorn, 2011). Students who have LD are challenged with learning, reading, writing, and math skills; have speech/language impairments, and have social skill deficits. Comorbid disorders include ADHD, ASD, Dyslexia, and Dyscalculia. LD is often treated by therapy and the use of medication. Teaching students with LD requires patience on the part of educators and the use of evidence-based practices.

Recommendations

For students with LD to achieve the most out of their learning experience, educators must thoroughly understand different learning disabilities and comorbid disorders associated with LD. Educators must be able to apply evidence-based practices that were learned during their training and teaching certification courses. For novice educators, there must be in-classroom hands-on training. Professional development must be on-going for all educators. Experienced educators must realize that best practices that were learned years ago may no longer be appropriate and are out-of-date in the modern-day classroom setting. Teaching pedagogies and classroom interventions are continuously changing to accommodate many ethnicities and diverse learners that was non-existent years ago. Educators must keep up-to-date in their profession.

Chapter 10
Misophonia

Introduction

Misophonia is part of sensory disorder that includes hyperosmia, tactile sensitivity, and misophonia. Misophonia may cause an unpleasant response to different sounds made by objects or other individuals like, a ticking pendulum in a clock, clicking of a pen, sniffing, tapping, or any repetitive noise. Different students who have misophonia will react dissimilarly to different sounds. These repetitive sounds can be antecedents to inappropriate behavior because the sound irritates students with misophonia in the classroom. Misophonia is or psychiatric disorder (American Psychiatric Association, 2013).

What Is Misophonia?

Students with misophonia are emotionally affected by sounds made by others. These sounds are ignored by others. The misophonic reaction is an uncontrolled somatic and emotional reaction triggered by sound when it enters and activates the Autonomic Nervous System. These sounds can cause anger or aggressive behaviors or a strong yearning to leave the area where the sound is originating (Cartreine, 2019). Misophonia is a serious disorder that hinders academic progress at school and social development that may lead to other health concerns. Misophonia manifests itself during the preteen years of most adolescents and does not disappear over time. The more often the sound is heard, the more the individual affected feels anger, hate, or rage. The characteristics of misophonia become more pronounced and stronger without treatment.

Characteristics/Traits

An individual with misophonia may exhibit disgust or an irritation that turns into anger. This behavior that is manifested may escalate into becoming aggressive toward the person creating the sound. Furthermore, the individual with misophonia may become physically aggressive by throwing objects and assaulting the person creating the sound. Students with misophonia generally realize that their responses to certain noises and sounds are extreme causing the intensity of their sensations may make them lose control. At first, the student may experience only one over-stimulus to a certain sound, but as the misophonia develops, the over-stimulus can expand to two or more sounds. Misophonia tends to develop in early teenage years of both boys and girls.

Comorbid Disabilities/Disorders

Some common comorbid disorders include Obsessive-Compulsive Disorder (OCD), neurodevelopmental conditions such as ADHD, ASD, and Fragile X syndrome. Misophonia, a neurophysiological disorder, has different clinical characteristics associated with other psychological disorders. It is important to understand the comorbidities to treat misophonia. According to Erfanian, Kartsonaki, and Keshavarz (2019), other disorders associated with misophonia include Major Depressive Disorder (MDD), OCD, and PTSD. MDD is when an adolescent is depressed most of the time, that can lead to lose of interest in school work and social activities.

The limbic system that is a group of interconnected structures located deep within the brain is the system that plays a role in anger and outside sensory stimuli, such as sounds. This part of the brain plays a role in behavioral and emotional responses. The amygdala is the part of the brain that processes long-term memories, fear, and where other emotions are activated. The amygdala is part of the limbic system. See Section I of the Appendix for approximate locations in the brain.

Treatments

Misophonia is a newly identified health disorder, and treatment options are still limited. According to the case study of Potgieter et al. (2019), treatments include cognitive behavioral rehabilitation, counterconditioning, mindfulness and acceptance, dialectical behavior therapy, and medications. Cognitive

Rehabilitation Therapy applies different treatment approaches that are intended to address challenges; attention, judgment, learning, memory, perception, and planning. These challenges can be caused by traumatic brain injury, neurological disorders, and other ailments. Counterconditioning is also known as stimulus substitution. This is part of applied behavior analysis that encompasses the conditioning of undesirable behavior and replacing it with a desired behavior or response correlated to a positive action with the stimulus. Mindfulness and acceptance therapy is teaching individuals about accepting the feelings and suffering that may take place after experiencing a bad circumstance or occurrence and learning how these feelings and suffering occur in our thoughts. Individuals learn through therapy sessions how to control and overcome the situation that causes these thoughts. This does not mean that the bad situation must be accepted; just the feelings must be acknowledged. Dialectical Behavior Therapy (DBT) is a cognitive-behavioral therapy that is a combination of mindfulness, acceptance, and emotion regulation therapies. DBT is an evidence-based psychotherapy used for personality disorders, suicidal tendencies, and for replacement of self-harm and substance abusebehaviors. Lastly, pharmaceutical approaches are also used to treat misophonia.

Medications

Currently, there is no cure or pharmaceutical treatment to overcome misophonia. Students are often prescribed drugs that treat comorbid mental health disorders. These include antidepressant or anti-anxiety drugs, including benzodiazepines, Xanax, Valium, buspirone (Buspar), and lorazepam (Ativan). Some individuals reported that taking antidepressant and anti-anxiety drugs helped. See Section II of the Appendix for List of Drugs with explanations of how they are used for treatment. Other individuals have reports that taking these drugs were a waste of time and did not help.

Teaching Students with Misophonia

Teaching students with misophonia can be challenging. Repetitive sounds can trigger unacceptable behaviors in the classroom and can hinder good classroom management. It has been suggested that students with misophonia be allowed to wear noise canceling headphones or ear pods. The other approach is allowing the student to go to a part of the room where the sound is less obtrusive. When the sound can be heard in every part of the classroom, the student may have to go to another room. These approaches may resolve the problem with the sound, but they will negatively impact the academic progress of the student because they may not be able to hear what the teacher is saying or attempting to explain in the classroom. If the student has services under special education and has an IEP, the student may be assigned alternate assignments that permit the student to work alone and have additional support in place. It should be noted that misophonia is not a qualifying disorder that will make that student eligible for services under special education (U.S. Dept. of Education, 2018). If the student is in special education because of a qualifying disorder such as ASD, ED/LD, ADHD, and misophonia as a comorbid disorder; the student will be entitled to receive appropriate for misophonia as well as other disorders.

Conclusions

Students with misophonia suffer because of a sensory over-stimulus. The repetitive sounds heard are exacerbating and irritative. Usually, misophonia is a comorbidity of other disorders like ASD, ED/LD, and ADHD. Psychological therapy is available for students in special education and can be mandated if student has had a multi-disciplinary evaluation team and is stipulated in the student IEP. It must be noted that misophonia is not one of the labels that IDEA legislation has indicated that must be diagnosed for services under special education. However, if misophonia is a comorbidity of one of the disorders listed in IDEA, the student may receive therapy. Many times, the therapy will encompass both the main label disorder, like autism and misophonia. Educators are challenged with the accommodations of these students in inclusive settings and self-contained classrooms.

Recommendations

It is important that educators understand that characteristics of misophonia and can take measures that will help the student overcome these sounds. This understanding will insure less student behavioral meltdowns, more student academic progress, and better classroom management. Training must be made available in college level certification courses as well as on-going professional development within private and public schools. Educators must be aware that every student is different and that a strategy or intervention that works well for one student may not work at all for another.

Chapter 11
Obsessive-Compulsive Disorder

Introduction

Obsessive-Compulsive Disorder (OCD) is a very common disorder in classrooms in both public and private schools. A student with OCD reacts to emotional stimuli that can lead to uncontrollable repetitive behaviors. Compulsions are behaviors that are learned and may become habitual and repetitive over time. The purpose of this chapter is to explore what causes OCD, its characteristics and traits, comorbid disorders, treatments, medications, and teaching students with OCD. OCD affects all socio-economic levels. OCD may appear in both affluent and impoverished, educated, and non-educated family members.

What is Obsessive-Compulsive Disorder (OCD)?

Obsessive-Compulsive Disorder (OCD) is an incapacitating cerebral disorder that involves stressful obsessions leading to repetitive compulsive behaviors. Researchers have been unable to locate the specific gene associated with OCD; although it is considered genetic, and twins have a higher risk of inheriting OCD. Obsessions are unintended thoughts or images that increase anxiety and fear that cause acting out of repetitive behaviors to relieve or decrease anxiety, uneasiness, or fear (Williams et al., 2017). Many of these behaviors occur when a person has ASD. Students with ASD will spend hours putting little figurines in order. Many times, they are worried about contamination and will refuse to put their hands into paper-mâché or something messy like mixing up food. Pacing and flapping are other examples of OCD.

Characteristics/Traits

Characteristics of OCD are behaviors including over-checking, mental contamination, Ordering and symmetry, intrusive thoughts, and hoarding. Over-checking involves the compulsive re-checking of one's work for fear something may not be right. Examples of mental contamination are taking a bath obsessive times during the day, obsessively washing hands, or fear of touching another person or object. Ordering or symmetry include obsessive neatness or lining up small objects in a certain order. Intrusive thoughts are repetitive feelings that can be disturbing, dreadful, and distasteful in nature. An example of OCD may be a person continuously thinking that another person will be killed in an accident (Mayo Clinic, 2021).

Many students develop unhealthy behaviors such as nail biting or teeth grinding, particularly during periods of high stress. In more severe cases and compared to OCD, Trichotillomania is manifested that is the compulsive urge to pull out (and possibly ingest) ones' own hair, including eyelashes and eyebrows (Arzeno Ferrao et al., 2006). Signs of OCD will begin to manifest themselves gradually and may fluctuate throughout life. What causes OCD is not known. According to research, there are several parts of the brain that are accountable. Parts of the brain that do not respond well to serotonin may cause OCD. It is thought that OCD may be genetic. There is a 25% chance that someone of the immediate family may have it (Paulis and Alsobrook, 1999). Lastly, many students with OCD also have other comorbid psychiatric disorders that must be addressed.

Comorbid Disabilities/Disorders

One of the main comorbid disorders correlated with OCD is ASD, including Asperger's. Many parents with ASD and OCD can be passed on to their offspring. The risk of having OCD and ASD in families is high (Meier et al., 2015). <u>Other comorbidities of OCD include ASD, ADHD, PTSD, Schizophrenia, and PDD-NOS</u>. Schizophrenia is a serious mental disorder and individuals with schizophrenia have 25% chance of having OCD. Many of the characteristics of the comorbid disorders are similar and others quite different. It is rare that students with OCD do not exhibit another comorbid disorder. Individuals with OCD will frequently exhibit other disorders as well (Pallanti et al., 2011). OCD cannot go on untreated because worsening conditions may result such as physical disorders and in rare cases, the individual with OCD may become suicidal.

It is thought that chemical changes in the body may be responsible for the pathogenesis of OCD. The parts of the brain affected by chemical changes in the body include the orbitofrontal and anterior cingulate cortices, basal ganglia, and thalamus (Mayo Clinic, 2021). See Section I of the Appendix for approximate locations in the brain. OCD is not a curable disorder, and it develops due to genetic factors.

Treatments

There are two treatment approaches used to treat OCD. These include psychotherapy and pharmaceutical drugs. Many times, both approaches are combined to obtain optimal results. Psychotherapy is effective in reducing obsessions and compulsions. CBT and exposure response therapy (ERT) are used. This therapy exposes the individual to a situation or stimulus that will provoke the obsessive-compulsive disorder. The exposure is controlled in a manner that will permit the individual to have less feeling of anxiety or distress toward the condition overtime. Antidepressant medications are used to help control the anxiety and distress associated with OCD.

Medications

Usually, antidepressant medications are used such as Selective Serotonin Reuptake Inhibitor (SSRI). See Section II of the Appendix for List of Drugs with explanations of how they are used for treatment. This approach helps reduce the individual's obsessions and compulsions and increase tolerance toward anxiety related to the obsessive thoughts. This therapy will help the person not act out the compulsive behavior. This can lead to overcoming the challenge with the compulsive behavior and may lead to self-mastery of the condition. Undergoing therapeutical and pharmaceutical treatments simultaneously has proven effective in helping individuals with OCD.

Teaching Students with OCD

Educators who are in a classroom with students with OCD will observe atypical behaviors that are strange and sometimes disruptive. Typical students will find these behaviors distract them from being focused on classroom academic activities. Examples of these behaviors include a student lining up little toy soldiers or engaging in self-injurious behaviors like pulling their hair out or students cutting themselves. Self-injurious behaviors are manifested when a student is angry or has anxiety. Other behaviors like pacing or flapping are compulsive behaviors associated with ASD.

There are strategies and evidence-based practices educators can use to teach students with OCD. Educators must have accommodations in place for these students and have a thorough understanding of this disorder as well as the atypical students. Educators are aware of evidence-based practices, but they must also receive assistance to help them implement strategies associated with evidence-based practices (Knight, Sartini, and Spriggs, 2015). Accommodations should be made to include students with OCD in group activities. These students should be part of a group of typical students who are understanding and well-behaved. If the student refuses to be part of a group, he or she should be allowed to do their work independently. The classroom assignments must be written, explained, and repeated until all the students understand.

Conclusions

A student with OCD reacts to emotional stimuli that can lead to uncontrollable repetitive behaviors. Compulsions are behaviors that are learned and may become habitual and repetitive over time (Williams et al., 2017). Comorbidities of OCD include ASD, ADHD, PTSD, Schizophrenia, and PDD-NOS. One of the main comorbid disorders correlated with OCD is ASD including Asperger's (Meier et al., 2015). The main treatments of OCD include psychotherapy and medication. Many times, both treatments are combined to obtain optimal results. Evidence-based practices should be in place for achieving best results when teaching these students in inclusive classroom settings and self-contained classrooms.

Recommendations

It is important to understand the characteristics and traits of OCD. Educators must get to know each student individually with OCD. Being aware of the student's life at home or outside the school environment is important. Evidenced-based practices must be in place in the classroom. Educators must be trained and have on-going professional development for how to apply strategies associated with evidence-based practices. Mentor teachers must provide hands-on training to especially novice teachers. During certification courses, novice teachers must participate in more hands-on and in-classroom training. Educators must understand evidence-based practices based on scientific research and be able to apply this knowledge.

Chapter 12
Oppositional Defiant Disorder

Introduction

Oppositional Defiant Disorder (ODD) is a behavior disorder that includes a persistent manifestation of hostile, malicious, and defiant behavior toward individuals that have authority. The student with ODD can become violent and be a danger to him/herself, other students, school administrators, and educators. The scope of this chapter will explore what ODD is, what are the causes, characteristics and traits, comorbidities, treatments available, and what strategies and interventions educators must have in place to successfully interact with and teach students with OCD.

What is Oppositional Defiant Disorder (ODD)?

This behavior often manifests itself in the preschool years. At first, it can be difficult to differentiate from developmentally appropriate, although troublesome, behavior (Hamilton and Armando, 2008). What causes ODD is unknown, but research indicates ODD is a combination of environmental and genetic influences. Environmental constraints include individual problems with parenting, lack of supervision, abuse, neglect, or severe discipline. Other family issues include mental health or substance abuse. Genetical constraints include neurobiological variances in the way the nerves and brain interact. Manifestations of ODD usually begin before a student is eight years old.

Criteria listed for diagnosing ODD is provided in *The Diagnostic and Statistical Manual of Mental* Disorders (DSM-5), published by the American Psychiatric Association. According to DSM-5, the individual must exhibit behavioral and emotional symptoms for at least six months (American Psychiatric Association, 2013). There is evidence that a reduced sensitivity to punishment and reward may exist. Research also indicates that the structure and function of the amygdala may be a causation of students exhibiting symptoms of ODD and other conduct problems with and without psychopathic conditions (Matthys, Vanderschuren, and Lochman, 2012).

Characteristics/Traits

Characteristics and traits of ODD include being angry and irritable, annoying other people, easily irritated by others, argumentative, losing temper, defiant, arguing with adults or authority figures, being physically and verbally aggressive, refusing to comply, breaking rules, blaming others for mistakes or inappropriate behavior, and vindictiveness. ODD can fluctuate in severity. Having mild symptoms, it can take place in only one location, like at home, school, work, or with peers. Moderate severity takes place in at least two locations. Severe ODD can occur in three or more locations (American Psychiatric Association, 2013). According to a study of Şener and Kilic (2005), other characteristics of ODD may include depression, delinquent and aggressive behavior, sex problems, and social problems. If the oppositional behaviors are provoked by others, the behavior manifested by the student may become physically and verbally violent. This escalation of behavior will become dangerous for the individual with ODD and others. The key is not allowing the escalation of the behavior to occur.

Comorbid Disabilities/Disorders

Comorbid disabilities and disorders include ADHD, ASD, Social Skill Deficit, ED/LD, Schizophrenia Spectrum Disorder (SSD), and Bipolar Disorders. Students who have ODD also can have ADHD and is a highly prevalent comorbidity. When diagnosed with both ADHD and ODD, the individual manifests more severe conditions associated with ADHD and ODD. When diagnosed with just ADHD or ODD, the conditions manifested are less severe (Noordermeer et al., 2017). According to a study of Simonoff et al. (2008), 28.1% of individuals diagnosed with ASD had ODD as a comorbid disorder. Other comorbid disorders associated with ODD include Social Skill Deficits, ED/LD, Bipolar Disorders, and Schizophrenia.

Having ODD will hinder that development of social skills and exacerbate ED/LD due to non-compliance with established behavioral norms. There is a genetic relationship between ODD and bipolar disorders (Azeredo, Moreira, and Barbosa, 2018). 84% of individuals diagnosed with schizophrenia were also diagnosed with ODD (Ross, Heinlein, and Tregellas, 2006). According to a meta-analysis study of neuroimaging using voxel-based morphometry, ODD may be caused by abnormally low gray matter development in the prefrontal cortex and in the left amygdala of the brain. See Section I of the Appendix for approximate locations in the brain. Early diagnosis leads to promising results when individuals with ODD participate in therapy and are treated (Rogers and De Brito, 2015). If there is an early diagnosis, treatment can begin at an earlier age. With earlier treatment, most students tend to make better progress in school in academic subjects as well as social skill development.

Treatments

Treatments for ODD include psychotherapy and pharmaceutical drugs. Many times, both approaches are combined to obtain optimal results. The treatments can be for ODD or for ODD and the comorbid disorders associated with ODD. These treatments include cognitive behavioral rehabilitation, counterconditioning, mindfulness and acceptance, and dialectical behavior therapy. At the onset of the diagnosis of ODD, therapy should begin. Early intervention will help the individual better control ODD in later life. Pharmaceutical approaches have also been successful in the treatment and control of ODD and associated comorbidities.

Medications

No medications have been FDA-approved for the treatment of ODD; however, antipsychotics, mood stabilizers are commonly prescribed to children with ODD for other comorbidities. These drugs include Aripiprazole (Ability) and Risperidone. These medications are prescribed to control aggressive behavior and anxiety. Side effects include dizziness and lightheadedness, and fainting. Ability is prescribed over Risperidone because of hormonal imbalances observed in males; such as, reduced testosterone levels and breast enlargement. Hormonal imbalances with the use of Abilify have also been observed. When used by females in some cases, Ability has caused an over-production of prolactin, a hormone-controlling milk production in mammals. Over production of milk is known as hyperprolactinemia.

Both Aripiprazole and Risperidone are effective in treating aggressive behaviors and mood disorder, but patients prescribed Aripiprazole have shown less of the above-mentioned side-effects. Placebos are also used to treat behavioral disorders; however, placebos contain no active ingredients other than glucose and sugar. One drug used called Obecalp is placebo spelled backwards. These drugs are used in conjunction with other psychotherapies. These are known as fake drugs and are prescribed to make the patient think their behavior has improved. These drugs look like other drugs, but they have no chemical properties that will influence behaviors associated with ODD or any of the comorbid disorders. With some individuals with ODD, these fake drugs have been effective. See Section II. of the Appendix for List of Drugs with explanations of how they are used for treatment.

Teaching Students with ODD

Educators who teach students with ODD and its comorbidities must have a lot of patience and endure a lot of verbal and sometimes physical abuse in the classroom. Because this stressful environment, many educators are unable to endure the elevated stress caused by the constant inappropriate behaviors of these students and end up resigning and leaving the teaching profession. Future special educators must be better prepared and must be better trained to interact and teach students with ODD and comorbid disorders. They must have hands-on classroom training as well as theoretical training and instruction. Seasoned general educators are now required to have these students in inclusive general education classroom settings. They must receive additional training and on-going professional development to be able to interact with and teach these students. Professional development and training for both general and special educators will help them apply evidence-based practices and intervention in the classroom.

Conclusions

Oppositional defiant disorder is a reoccurring pattern of developmentally unsuitable, pessimistic, defiant, and disobedient behavior toward authority figures (Hamilton and Armando, 2008). Characteristics and traits of ODD include being angry and irritable, annoying other people, easily irritated by others, argumentative
, losing temper, defiant, arguing with adults or authority figures, being physically and verbally aggressive, refusing to comply, breaking rules, blaming others for mistakes or inappropriate behavior, and vindictiveness.

Comorbid disabilities and disorders include ADHD, ASD, Social Skill Deficit, ED/LD, Schizophrenia Spectrum Disorder (SSD), and Bipolar Disorders. Treatments for ODD include psychotherapy and pharmaceutical drugs. Many times, both approaches are combined to obtain optimal results. Both general and special educators must be prepared to interact and teach students of ODD. The inappropriate behavior of these students is a major cause of educators leaving the teaching profession.

Recommendations

Thoroughly understanding the nature of ODD is extremely important and will make a difference in classroom management and the longevity of time in the teaching profession. Being able to understand the students' reasons for the behavioral meltdown will assist the educator in being able to diffuse the inappropriate behavior. ODD is believed to be caused by genetic irregularities but can be exacerbated by environmental occurrences. An abusive home environment can be that cause of violent in-school behavior and non-compliance with authority figures. As with most other student disabilities and disorders, both general and special educators must have appropriate training and on-going professional development to interact with students with ODD.

Chapter 13
Photophobia

Introduction

Photophobia is sensory disorder caused by over-stimuli of the senses. Other sensory disorders caused by over-stimuli include hyperosmia, misophonia and tactile dysfunction. Literally, photophobia is made up of two Greek works that mean light (photo) and fear (phobia) but in the case of this disorder, it is not a fear of the light but a discomfort due to over-sensitivity to light or types of light, pulsing light, and colors. This chapter will focus on the causes of photophobia, comorbid disorders, treatments, medications, and what is needed to teach students suffering from photophobia in the classroom. Many times, sensitivity to the light is often overlooked and not understood.

What is Photophobia?

Photophobia is a sensory disorder that is triggered by light that causes discomfort in the eye or head. Individuals with photophobia may be more comfortable is a darkened room or use sunglasses indoors. Students have photophobia because of different medical circumstances, eye conditions, central nervous system disorders, and psychiatric conditions (Wu and Hallett, 2017). These conditions can be genetical. Photophobia can be provoked by a traumatic brain injury (TBI). Individuals who have suffered a fall, concussion, or other traumatic brain injury can experience photophobia as well. Photophobia can be drug-induced as well. Medications that are responsible include barbiturates, benzodiazepines, and haloperidol (Wu and Hallett, 2017). These drugs are used to control and treat other psychological disorders.

Characteristics/Traits

Some characteristics that individuals with photophobia experience include migraine headaches, nausea, blurred vision, pain in the eye or head, and additional traits due to other eye diseases. Migraine and other types of headaches are experienced by 80% to 90% of individuals affected by photophobia. These headaches usually occur simultaneously with the individual's exposure to light but can occur at other times with no exposure to light. Photophobia causes vestibular symptoms that include nausea, lightheadedness, and dizziness. Pain in the head or eye can be caused by a primary, migraine, tension, or cluster headache. A cluster headache is characterized by severe burning and intense pain.

Comorbid Disabilities/Disorders

Psychiatric comorbidities associated with photophobia include depression, anxiety, bipolar disorder, epilepsy, seizures, ADHD, and ASD. Individuals who have psychological conditions are more prone to having photophobia. Depression and anxiety can be exacerbated by headaches that are a common trait of photophobia. Epilepsy and seizures can be provoked by flashing or pulsating light. These conditions can be uncomfortable and lead to a seizure (Wu and Hallett, 2017). Students who have been diagnosed with ADHD and ASD have a higher prevalence of photophobia. Photophobia is a symptom of one or more problems. For example, light sensitivity may be caused by photoreceptors in the retina, the rods and cones, ganglion cells, optic nerves, thalamus region of the brain, and somatosensory center in the cortex. See Section I of the Appendix for approximate locations in the brain. Treatment for photophobia and other psychiatric ailments are similar and may occur simultaneously.

Treatments

Most treatments for photophobia may be psychotherapy or by pharmaceutical means. These treatments may be combined therapy and medication or may be separate. Normally, the treatment for headaches associated with photophobia is by drugs. For the treatment and control of light irritation, different types of glasses are prescribed. These include glasses with sunlight and glare protection, sunglasses, pinhole glasses, and inside tinted glasses. The type of glass prescribed will depend on the level of photophobia experienced by the student. The glasses are intended to reduce light sensitivity and reduce the occurrence of headaches. Most of the therapy for photophobia occurs in conjunction with the therapy for the comorbid disorders experienced by the student.

Medications

Treatments for headaches associated with photophobia are usually controlled by migraine beta-blockers, Aspirin, Ibuprofen, or Excedrin. Blurred vision is treated separately. Other medications prescribed for photophobia include eyedrops the reduce eye irritation, redness, and inflammation. Medications for artificial tears and antibiotic eyedrops are prescribed for corneal abrasions. See Section II of the Appendix for List of Drugs with explanations of how they are used for treatment. If the student is given medication and is receiving therapy at the same time; the other medications prescribed will align with what is best for the comorbid disorder like ASD, ADHD, epilepsy, or bipolar disorders as well as photophobia. These medications were mentioned in previous chapters.

Teaching Students with Photophobia

Teaching students with photophobia is less challenging if educators understand photophobia and have accommodations in place in the classroom for students with photophobia. Anti-glare monitors are very important as well as being able to adjust the brightness intensity. However, educators must be aware that most of the time, there are other comorbidities that must be considered. In addition to the accommodations in place for photophobia, there must be other accommodations that align with the other disorders. Evidence-based practices used for other classroom disabilities and disorders should be in place as mentioned in earlier chapters. These practices will reduce frustrations, student meltdowns, improve classroom management, and the overall academic achievement of these students.

Conclusions

Photophobia is a sensory disorder that can be uncomfortable to painful. If classroom accommodations are not in place; this condition can lead to inappropriate classroom behavior that may be disruptive or violent. Uncomfortable or painful circumstances can be easily mitigated with the use of darkened glasses, glare-free computer monitors, or reduced exposure to bright light, different colors, or pulsating flashes of light. Educators must be mindful that photophobia can have comorbidities that have behavioral characteristics that they must be able to confront as well. These comorbidities are other disorders that must be dealt with by using other strategies and accommodations in conjunction to those used for photophobia. Educators that have a thorough knowledge of how to confront challenges with photophobia and other comorbid disorders will bring about a greater degree of success with the students.

Recommendations

Confronting student challenges with photophobiaand having in place the proper accommodations to mitigate these challenges will bring about improved classroom management and improved learning in the classroom. Educators must interact with students with photophobia with an open mind and realize that every student will react to photophobia in different ways. How students react to their condition will depend on their other comorbid disorders and cognitive level. Utilizing evidence-based practices in the classroom have been found to be the most effective when teaching both typical and atypical students. UDL and UbD are two teaching models that have been found effective in the classroom. Universal Design for Learning (UDL) focuses on the learning needs of students as a top priority. Understanding by Design (UbD) emphasizes goals and how and what should be learned while using a backward approach to achieve those goals. Educators should learn and apply both UDL and UbD to see which model works best in their classroom.

Chapter 14
Rett Syndrome

Introduction

This chapter will explore Rett Syndrome. This rare genetic mutation affects brain development and is more common in girls than in boys. There are fewer than 1,000 cases per year in the United States. It is worth mentioning because at least once or twice, educators will experience a student with Rett Syndrome in their school. The causes of Rett Syndrome, comorbid disorders, treatments, medications, and what is needed to teach students suffering from Rett Syndrome will be covered in this section. Because of its rarity, this condition is barely understood by educators.

What is Rett Syndrome?

Rett syndrome is a neurodevelopmental disorder that is considered as ASD. Both Rett Syndrome and ASD are neurodevelopmental disorders. It is categorized as an autism spectrum disorder, but, unlike most forms of autism, Rett Syndrome is different because the cause is due to a mutation in a protein known as MeCP2. Some differences between ASD and Rett Syndrome is that autism can be diagnosed at birth, but Rett Syndrome is diagnosed about 6 to 18 months after birth. Rett Syndrome affects more girls than boys. ASD affects more boys than girls and the degree of severity can change as the person gets older. Some students with ASD improve and appear to overcome traits associated with ASD. Rett Syndrome is progressive, and those individuals affected will begin to lose motor skill coordination and speech (Neul, 2012). Rett Syndrome is genetic, but it cannot be inherited.

There are four stages of Rett Syndrome. Stage one is when the early onset of this disorder occurs between 6 and 18 months. Some developmental milestones may not be met. Stage two is a rapid regression period, roughly between 1 and 4 years old. Fine and Gross motor skills and speech/language skills decline. Stage three is when the conditions of Rett Syndrome stabilize or plateau. This state can last for years. Finally, state four is when the person loses motor skills, becomes deficient in most movements. Muscles become weak and joints become stiff. This stage can begin at 5 and last till after 25 years old. These times in years will vary among different individuals.

Characteristics/Traits

Characteristics and traits associated with Rett Syndrome are abnormalities with gross and fine motor skills. Students with Rett Syndrome may need assistance walking or be confined to a wheelchair and will have difficulty holding a pencil. Individuals tend to be shorter in height for their age. Many have gastrointestinal problems that causes chewing and swallowing challenges, gastroesophageal reflux, bloating, and bowel movement problems. Hyperventilation, seizures, cardiovascular disease, and behavioral manifestations like ASD also occur. These behaviors include withdrawal from social events, speech/language disorders, and avoidance of eye contact. Diagnosis of ASD is more prevalent if Rett Syndrome and is less severe. Many times, those individuals initially diagnosed with ASD may be re-diagnosed to Rett Syndrome later.

Comorbid Disabilities/Disorders

Comorbidities with Rett Syndrome include dysphagia and sleep disorders. There is a multisystem of comorbidities across all relevant organ systems. Some individuals with Rett Syndrome have cardiovascular concerns. Social Skill Deficits, Speech/Language, and gross and fine motor skills are common comorbid disorders with Rett Syndrome.

Rett Syndrome is caused by the mutation of the MeCP2 gene in the X chromosome. The mutation takes place because there are changes in protein. There are more than 900 different mutations found in this gene (Neul, 2012). These genetic mutations affect brain development. Regions of the brain affected include the reduction of dorsal parietal gray matter and the preservation of the occipital cortex. See Section I of the Appendix for approximate locations in the brain. There is an overall brain volume reduction (Carter, 2008).

Treatment

There is no known cure for Rett Syndrome, but medications are available, physical, speech/language therapy, and dietary support can control symptoms, prevent complications, and enhance quality of life. Occupational therapists will help students with fine and gross motor skills deficiencies using everyday activities. Muscle strength and tone are improved through exercises such as walking and learning to use a pencil to write. Speech and language pathologists will emphasize enhancing, supporting, and developing the communication skills of individuals with Rett Syndrome. To improve receptive and expressive communication, augmentative communication devices may be used in place of speech for non-verbal students. Dietary support is important for students with Rett Syndrome. A special, well-balanced diet is developed to support the needs of individuals with port growth and weight gain (Leonard et al., 2013). Therapy is very affective in maintaining everyday life skills for students with Rett Syndrome, but medication has also proven successful.

Medications

Drugs used to treat seizures in students with Rett Syndrome include lamotrigine, levetiracetam, oxcarbazepine, and valproic acid. Antidepressant desipramine improved respiratory rhythm. Research continues to study new types of drugs to enhance motor skill development. On the average, most individuals with the conditions can live until 40 or 50 years old (Chapleau, 2013). Clenbuterol, an asthma drug, may prove successful in building muscles and help develop motor skills in individuals with Rett Syndrome. See Section II. of the Appendix for List of Drugs with explanations of how they are used for treatment. The future looks bright for new medications on the horizon.

Teaching Students with Rett Syndrome

Seeing students in the classroom who are non-verbal, with severe motor skill deficits, and appearing to regress as the years pass can be sad, frustrating, and insurmountable for most educators. Educators want to be able to help, but how? Educators can use specific interventions to help these students. The use of augmentative communication devices can prove successful. Games can be used to help with motor skills as well as teaching basic math, reading, and writing skills. Use of visuals, manipulatives, music therapy, and toys can also be helpful. These interventions must be tailored to fit the individual need of students according to their different cognitive levels. Instruction must be individualized (Katsiyannis et al., 2001).

Conclusions

Rett Syndrome is a rare disorder that is not well understood by educators. Students with this disorder manifest symptoms of physical and behavioral difficulties, and delays in normal development. Comorbidities with Rett Syndrome are lifelong and genetic. Brain development is hindered because of genetic mutations. Treatment is available with therapy and medications. Both psychotherapy and pharmaceutical solutions can be used simultaneously. Teaching students with Rett Syndrome can be overwhelming, but with the use of manipulatives, visuals, games, and one-on-one support, some progress can be made even though the disorder is progressive and those individuals with Rett Syndrome can regress or plateau over time.

Recommendations

Educators, administrators, and paraprofessional who interact, teach, and support students with Rett Syndrome need additional training and professional development. Since the disorder is rare, it is often overlooked in teacher certification classes and training. Many students with Rett Syndrome are relegated to self-contained classrooms; however, some of these students make it into general education classroom settings. Educators as well as therapists should use evidence-based practices in the classroom for best results.

Chapter 15
Schizophrenia

Introduction

Schizophrenia is a pervasive developmental disorder. Schizophrenia is a serious condition that affects that way an individual thinks, feels, and behaves. The intent of this chapter is to focus on the causes of schizophrenia, its comorbid disorders, treatments, medications, and what is needed to teach students suffering from schizophrenia in the classroom. Many comorbid disorders include many of the same disorders that were covered in previous chapters. Treatments and medications vary depending on the individual and severity of the disorder. Teaching students with schizophrenia can be challenging for educators who have little experience interacting with students with pervasive developmental disorders

What is Schizophrenia?

Schizophrenia is a grave mental illness characterized by disjointed or irrational thoughts, inexplicable behavior and speech, and delusions or hallucinations, such as hearing voices or thinking someone will do harm (American Psychiatric Association, 2013). Individuals with schizophrenia are challenged in beginning and preserving relationships as they are challenged with distortions of reality and are less able to integrate and unify thoughts. Schizophrenia is part of a family of five main pervasive developmental disorders including Autism and Asperger's Disorder (ASD), Childhood Disintegrative Disorder and Pervasive

Developmental Disorder Not Otherwise Specified (PDD-NOS), and Rett's Disorder. Many characteristics of these other disorders are like schizophrenia and have many of the same comorbidities. What distinguishes schizophrenia from other disorders is when individuals manifest delusional or hallucinatory behaviors. For example, Schizo-affective disorder is when an individual feels disconnected from reality that affects one's mood. This disorder develops between 16 and 30 years old.

Initially, schizophrenia was divided into two main types that included extreme paranoid and catatonic types. According to DSM-5 published by American Psychiatric Association (2013), these types are no longer considered subgroups. Individuals are now diagnosed as having schizophrenia exhibiting paranoid or positive symptoms. Extreme paranoid schizophrenia is when an individual has delusions of persecution, people wanting to harm, exaggerated thoughts of being famous, having extreme power with little support for these ideas. Catatonic schizophrenia is when individuals exhibit significant decrease in movement or hyperactivity Some individuals will assume postures as like a statue.

Characteristics/Traits

Two main characteristics of schizophrenia are manifestations of delusions and hallucinations. Delusional behaviors include the belief that the individual with schizophrenia is being manipulated by an outside force, such as a supernatural power or extraterrestrial. Persons believe that they possess a superpower or are a famous person. They are extremely jealous of their partner or spouse. They feel they are being mistreated or victimized. Individuals often believe that their mind is being controlled by some outside source.

Hallucinatory behaviors are caused by false sensory perceptions. Hearing voices is very common and are interpreted to be spiritual. Individuals may claim to see false images and can be very persuasive when telling others about what they see, like bodies or faces. Certain smells may haunt them. They may smell a food that used to be prepared by a dead relative.

What causes schizophrenia is unknown but is a genetical developmental disorder. Some other factors that may be responsible for emergence of schizophrenia include combination of genetic, physical, psychological, and environmental factors (Angermeyer and Hatschinger, 1996). Children younger than in their teenage years rarely develop schizophrenia.

Comorbid Disabilities/Disorders

According to a study of Karatzias et al. (2007), some common comorbidities associated with schizophrenia include anxiety, social anxiety disorder, alienation, social isolation, inability to feel pleasure (anhedonia), OCD, and blunted affect. Blunted affect refers to challenges expressing emotions, gesturing, and vocal response to reaction to an irritating stimulus. In some cases, comorbid disorders are absent when a person has schizophrenia. Many individuals with schizophrenia have expressed fear of their disorder and the inability to control it. Students may develop disorganized speech and will be challenged responding to questions. They may respond to questions with unrelated answers. Disorganized speech/language will lead to social skills deficits as well and will hinder a student's academic progress as well.

Abnormal structural connectivity in the prefrontal and medial temporal lobe of the brain may exacerbate the emergence of schizophrenia. See Section I of the Appendix for approximate locations in the brain. Because the brain of children in their early teens is still developing in these regions, development of schizophrenia occurs in late adolescent years of teenagers (Karlsgodt, Sun, and Cannon, 2010). Schizophrenia is a lifelong disorder with no cure but can be controlled through treatments.

Treatments

Both psychosocial and pharmaceutical interventions are used to control schizophrenia. This section will focus on psychosocial treatments available. Individual therapy is available to help control thought patterns of delusions, of hallucinations that lead to inappropriate behavior. Persons with schizophrenia are taught to cope with stress, lack of self-esteem, and anxiety. Usually, a trained psychiatrist, psychologist, behavioralist, or clinical worker will be responsible for leading these therapy sessions. In addition, a licensed social worker, speech-language therapist pathologist will be involved in therapy designed to improved community and social interaction. This therapy helps develop overall language skills that will help social interaction with others. Therapy helping individuals reconnect with reality is designed for schizo-affective disorders. Group therapy including others with schizophrenia and family members is focused on providing education concerning schizophrenia. Vocational rehabilitation is available to help students prepare for gainful employment, find, and keep jobs (Mayo Clinic, 2021). Treatments involving both therapy and drugs may be used simultaneously.

When an individual is exhibiting severe symptoms, hospitalization may be necessary. Many times, individuals may refuse, and under severe circumstances, to be hospitalized, claiming everything is "normal" with them. In these cases, they may be "Baker Acted" and taken to a mental care facility against their will. The Baker Act originated in Florida and has been applied when a person may cause harm to self or other individuals (Family Center for Recovery, 2021). There are other regions of the United States where similar legislation exists and is applied under similar circumstances. Electroconvulsive Therapy (ECT) is available in severe cases when individuals do not respond to drug treatments. ECT is given to a patient under general anesthesia when small amounts of electrical current are passed through the brain.

Medications

Second-generation antipsychotic drugs are suggested for use because of posing less side-effects. These drugs include Abilify, Saphris, Latuda, and Risperdal. They come in tablets or injectable forms. These drugs are not completely free of side-effects. There are long-lasting antipsychotic drugs that can be given by injection. See Section II of the Appendix for List of Drugs with explanations of how they are used for treatment. A problem with individuals who have schizophrenia is after taking these drugs, they feel better without symptoms of schizophrenia. They claim that having further treatment or taking these drugs is no longer necessary because they no longer have schizophrenia. A relapse will occur and a regression to the former state of schizophrenia will reappear. Schizophrenia is a lifelong condition and will not go away with age. On-going treatment and medication must continue through one's lifetime. Left untreated, schizophrenia will negatively influence all aspects of one's life.

Teaching Students with Schizophrenia

Teaching students with schizophrenia can be challenging for a novice teacher but with proper training, teaching this population of students is manageable. To be successful in teaching students with schizophrenia, educators must thoroughly understand this disorder and be aware of possible treatments students can receive. The classroom goals that are set for this population of students must be realistic academic and social goals. These goals differ among students and depend on the severity of the disorder. Many of the same strategies and interventions are the same as for students with other disabilities. Strategies may not be equally affective for all students. It is imperative that educators have a good rapport with parents and caregivers of these students. Establishing times for regular meetings with both the student and parents will help improve academic as well has social skill progress.

Conclusions

Schizophrenia is a genetic disorder that has various degrees of severity. Every student is dissimilar and will exhibit different traits and may have one or more comorbid disorders and disabilities as well. Some of the characteristics of schizophrenia are like other disorders such as ASD. The main distinguishing point between ASD and schizophrenia is that students with schizophrenia can be delusional and hallucinatory. These students imagine different things and events and are very convincing and persuasive in how they explain in what they see, feel, or hear. Both disorders have social skills deficits, speech/language disorders, and behavioral constraints. Students may also manifest ODD or OCD. Psychosocial and pharmaceutical interventions are available to treat and control schizophrenia. Educators who possess a thorough knowledge of schizophrenia will be in a better position to help these students and increase their academic and social skills progress.

Recommendations

Educators must have a thorough knowledge of schizophrenia and be able to have appropriate classroom accommodations in place to increase the academic progress of this population of students. Educators must have an open mind and understand that no two students with schizophrenia are the same. Many students having different comorbidities will react to situations in dissimilar ways. The severity of the disorder will influence how the student reacts and behaves. Additional training and professional development are strongly encouraged for educators. Utilizing evidence-based practices in the classroom have been found to be the most effective when teaching students with other disorders and without disorders.

Chapter 16
Self-Injurious Behavior

Introduction

Self-Injurious Behavior (SIB) is a common comorbid disorder with many other disorders and disabilities. It is very common among students with ASD, ODD, ID, and speech/language disorders. The focus of this chapter will focus on the causes of self-injurious behavior, comorbid disorders, treatments, medications, and what is needed to teach students with SIB in the classroom. Educators must be able to intervene when a student begins to manifest SIB because injuries self-inflicted by the student can be serious and become fatal in less-common occurrences.

What is Self-Injurious Behavior?

Self-Injurious Behavior (SIB) is a behavior in which an individual harms (or attempts to harm) oneself intentionally and physically (Van den Bogaard, Nijman, Palmstierna, and Embregts, 2018). Self-injurious behavior (SIB) is manifested by students with ASD and ID that involves inappropriate behavior that results in the self-infliction of physical injury to one's own body. SIB can be triggered by anger, emotional evocation or agitation, inability to process negative effects, and to relieve negative emotions (Son, Kim, and Lee, (2021). For some students with ASD, SIB can be a way to mediate discomfort by stimulating another discomfort or pain such as a headache. Also, SIB is a way to regulate sensory over-stimulus such as misophonia. SIB is genetic but can be induced by drugs. Students use SIB to help mitigate negative emotions (Muehlenkamp, 2005). There is no cure for SIB, but psychotherapy is available and is very helpful in most cases. Many teens overcome SIB and 90% of young adults do not report further symptoms of SIB after years of therapy (Melina, 2011).

Characteristics/Traits

Traits manifested by those affected by SIB include cutting, burning, head-banging, hitting. These usually occur in the front areas of the body. These characteristics are manifested to get out of a classroom activity the student does not like or to get attention (Muehlenkamp, 2005). Often, adolescents with self-injurious behavior have traumatic childhoods due to deficits in parenting, illness, or disability of another family member. Other traits include breaking bones, injecting toxins, or ingesting poisonous substances. Abuse of alcohol and drugs can exacerbate SIB (Conterio et al., 1998). It is not uncommon for an individual with self-injurious behavior to have an obsessive need to be a perfectionist and have a misperception of one or more aspects of one's own body (Stone and Sias, 2003).

Comorbid Disabilities/Disorders

Comorbidities include ASD, ID, ODD, and speech/language disorders. Students who have one or more of these disorders can also manifest SIB. Self-injurious behavior (SIB) is manifested by students with ASD and ID that involves inappropriate behavior that results in the self-infliction of physical injury to one's own body. Individuals with ASD have a higher probability of developing SIB when compared to individuals who have speech/language impairment. SIB is correlated to a variety of negative consequences that students endure with autism. These include head banging, self-biting, skin-picking, and self-hitting. Adolescents who exhibit ASD, may have chronic occurrences of SIB and other developmental disabilities (Minshawi et al., 2014).

SIB can be exhibited by students who have ID. There is a correlation between SIB and ID. Students that manifest more severe SIB will also manifest more severe ID. The incidence of severe self-injury in individuals with severe intellectual disability is approximately 5% (Oliver, License, and Richards, 2017). There is a positive association between SIB and OCC. Girls with antisocial personality disorders have a higher occurrence of SIB with suicidal tendencies (Crowell et al., 2005). Variations in the development of the left posterior cingulate cortex, right amygdala, left hippocampus, and right thalamus is responsible for the pathogenesis of SIB. See Section I of the Appendix for approximate locations in the brain. SIB is considered a genetic disorder.

Treatments

Both psychosocial and pharmaceutical interventions are used to control self-injurious behavior. Controlled psychotherapeutic interventions including collaborative associations, and motivation to replace SIB are available. Drugs that have been used target the serotonergic, dopaminergic, and opioid systems of the brain. These approaches have been used either with or without cognitive-behavioral therapy (CBT) (Turner, Austin, Chapman, 2014). CBT targets inappropriate behaviors to replace these behaviors with appropriate behaviors. Therapy sessions are offered by psychologists, psychiatrists, behavioralists, and social workers. The degree of SIB and other comorbidities will determine the professional responsible for the therapy.

Medications

SIB that is treated with antidepressants, antipsychotics, and mood stabilizers has mitigated the episodes of manifestations of this behavior (Smith, 2005). Antidepressant drugs include Celexa, Paxil, Prozac, and Zoloft. Antipsychotic drugs include Risperidone, Seroquel, Abilify, and Clozaril. Mood stabilizers used to treat SIB are Carbamazepine, Depakote, Lamotrigine, Lithium, and Depakene. Many of these drugs are used to treat other disorders mentioned in this book. All these drugs have side effects and the mental health care professional prescribing these drugs should understand that the effectiveness will vary and be different among different individuals.See Section II of the Appendix for List of Drugs with explanations of how they are used for treatment.

Teaching Students with Self-Injurious Behavior

Self-injurious behavior is one of the most confounding and interesting behaviors that educators, school psychologists, and counseling staff encounter in schools across the country. When students exhibit SIB, their bodies generate naturally produced endorphins that protect them from physical pain. Once self-injurious students have been identified, a male-female support group must be set up including educators who have students with SIB, psychologists, and counselors. They must understand the difference between SIB and suicidal behavior. School staff and faculty must be ready to use evidence-based practices to confront SIB constructively to mitigate this behavior. Students must be taught to cope with this behavior and use their protective defenses against it. Adults who respond to these students must be able to help them de-escalate SIB and protect them (Selekman, 2010).

Conclusions

Self-Injurious Behavior (SIB) is a genetic disorder that varies from student to student. Students who exhibit SIB will intentionally injure themselves to relieve their stress, anxiety, or other pain. Comorbidities include ASD, ID, ODD, and speech/language disorders. Both therapy and pharmaceutical treatments are available. School staff and faculty who interact with students having SIB must be aware of this disorder and be able to tell the difference between suicidal behavior. School personnel who are better prepared to deal with SIB will be in a better position to de-escalate the behavior of a student manifesting SIB and mitigate the degree of the self-injuries.

Recommendations

Preparedness is the best practice to confronting SIB. Professional development and training is recommended for all school personnel that will teach, counsel, or interact with these students. The use of evidence-based practices in the classroom have been found to be the most effective when teaching students with SIB. Normally students with SIB have other disorders as well and have an IEP. Educators and others should go over the IEP and understand what interventions and strategies have been put into place for the student. In addition, educators must converse with the parents or guardians of these students to find out more information about the student. This knowledge will be helpful when students exhibit SIB. Educators should build a good rapport with these students so trust will be present between the students and educators.

Chapter 17
Antisocial Personality Disorders

Introduction

Social Pathology and Psychopathology are Antisocial Personality Disorders with many differences and similarities. The scope of this chapter will compare these two disorders; what they are and are not, characteristics and traits, comorbid disorders, treatments and medications available, and teaching students in the classroom with these disorders. Educators must see when a student is exhibiting behaviors of social pathology or psychopathology and be able to intervene when other students are being taken advantage of. Commonly, individuals with these disorders are referenced to as sociopaths and psychopaths.

What is an Antisocial Personality Disorder?

There are two types of antisocial personality disorders that will be explored. Social pathology and sociopathology are the consequence of interaction between genetic and environment factors. Social pathology and psychopathology are not synonymous (Werner, Few, and Bucholz, 2015). An individual who is considered a social path manifests antisocial behavior that is caused by a way of believing, home environment, and/or brain injury. An individual who is a psychopath is thought to have acquired the disorder through genetic heredity. These two disorders are referred to as Antisocial Personality Disorders in the *Diagnostic and Statistical Manual of Mental Disorders* (DSM). Sociopaths have comparatively normal temperaments; their personality disorder affected by negative sociological considerations like parental neglect, friendships with delinquent peers, poverty, and extremely low or extremely high cognitive levels. Psychopaths tend to be more manipulative, can be seen by others as more charismatic, charming, appear to lead a normal life, and minimize their risk of being caught in criminal activities.

Characteristics/Traits

A comparison between psychopaths and social paths will be explored. Both psychopaths and social paths have antisocial personality disorder. Psychopaths may lack empathy and can be delusional (Dittrick et al., 2020). Psychologists generally consider psychopathy to be genetic or innate and social pathology to be caused by environmental factors or a combination of genetic and environmental factors. Psychopaths do not decide on impulse; they normally will plan out their schemes and are meticulous in planning their crimes. Social paths act on high impulsiveness. Crimes committed by psychopaths are usually premeditated with calculated risks.

Social paths commit crimes by taking high risks and do not plan. They will leave clues to the crime they committed and are easily caught. Psychopaths will use friendships to benefit themselves. They will have their family or friends do their dishonest or criminal tasks and when their friends get caught, the psychopath will not feel any remorse or empathy toward the individuals who carried out the illegal act (Tone and Tully, 2015). They tend to engage in white-collar crime like fraud. A social path, on the other hand, will empathize with the friends or family they hurt and will feel guilty.

Psychopaths often have successful careers. They try to establish trust between them and coworkers and bosses. To be successful, psychopaths will start false rumors in the workplace or uses others to get ahead. Social paths generally find it difficult to hold down a job because of impulsivity and erratic or unplanned bursts of violence. Both psychopaths and social paths commit crime because they are motivated by greed or revenge, except that the psychopath meticulously plans the crime, and the social path commits the crime on impulse.

Comorbid Disabilities/Disorders

There are several comorbidities manifested by adolescents and adults with antisocial personality disorder. These include suicidal ideation, nicotine dependence, alcohol and drug abuse, and anxiety (Werner, Few, Bucholz, 2015). According to a study of Moran and Hodgins (2004) ADHD, schizophrenia, and bipolar disorders are prevalent comorbid disorders in individuals who have both psychopathologic and social pathological disorders.

Individuals with antisocial personality disorder are unique because personality encompasses behaviors and emotions combined. Personality begins to form during early childhood and is an interaction of inherited constraints and environmental factors. The exact causation of antisocial personality disorder is not known, but it is caused by genetical factors. During the development of the brain, changes occur. Regions of the brain affected are in the prefrontal cortex, superior temporal gyrus, amygdala-hippocampal complex, and the anterior cingulate cortex (Yang, Glenn, Raine, 2008). See Section I of the Appendix for approximate locations in the brain. There are treatments available to mitigate to traits of antisocial personality disorder.

Treatments

Two therapies that showed effectiveness in treating antisocial behavior disorder are cognitive behavior therapy (CBT) and contingency management. CBT is a short-term, goal-oriented psychotherapy treatment that uses an applied or practical method for problem-solving. The goal of this therapy is to change the way someone thinks or behaves that is responsible for the individual's difficulties, and ultimately change the way the person feels. Changing the way someone thinks is a dauting task and can require long-term therapy for some. It is used to help treat a wide range of concerns in a person's life; from sleeping challenges or relationship constraints to drug and alcohol abuse or anxiety and depression. CBT works by changing people's attitudes and their behavior by focusing on the thoughts, viewpoints, images, and attitudes that are held, or how a person gains knowledge and stores information, and how these processes connect to the manner a person behaves, as a way of dealing with emotional issues (Matthys and Schutter, 2021).

Contingency management is a behavioral intervention commonly for individuals with drug abuse problems. This strategy focuses on promoting positive behavior replacement, such as abstinence, by introducing support when the individuals meet their goals during therapy and withholding support or introducing a punishment when individuals manifest an undesired behavior. Adolescents with antisocial behaviors responded well to CBT. Adolescents who underwent CBT when they were institutionalized manifested less criminal behavior during the first year after their release (Hunnikin et al., 2020).

Medications

Studies have shown little effectiveness when using drugs alone or used in conjunction with therapy to control Sociopathy and Psychopathology. The conclusion of a recent study of Khalifa et al. (2020) indicated that after participants were given Amantadine (dopamine agonist), Bromocriptine (dopamine agonist), Desipramine (antidepressant), Nortriptyline (antidepressant), and Phenytoin (antiepileptic), there was little effectiveness in reducing the traits of these areas of antisocial behavior disorder. See Section II. of the Appendix for List of Drugs with explanations of how they are used for treatment. There is no known medication that can mitigate the urges of a psychopath to engage in violent behavior or commit murder. Individuals with both sociopathy and psychopathology benefited from CBT and contingency behavior management. Long-term CBT of five years or more has shown reduction of violent and criminal behaviors of a psychopath.

Teaching Students with Social Pathology and Psychopathology

School districts across the country have instituted zero-tolerance policies to control inappropriate student behaviors. For the most part, these policies are ineffective. Suspensions are unproductive and detentions can exacerbate inappropriate student behavior. Students are not born with a preformed collection of aggressive behaviors. These behaviors are learned. Positive behavior support must be initiated and used throughout the entire school. There must be an ongoing formative data collection and monitoring of students exhibiting antisocial behaviors. Interaction with the social environment is needed to control unwanted learning of aggressive behaviors. Sources of this learning are from television, videos, games, antisocial peer groups, and home.

Positive behavior support is divided into three levels, including intensive intervention of one to five percent of the students with severe antisocial behaviors, targeted intervention for five to ten percent of the students with mild inappropriate behaviors, and universal intervention for all students or 80 to 90% of those not in the first two levels of the interventions. Student behavior should be monitored in the classroom, busses, hallways, lunchroom, and playground. Communication is necessary with the student's parents or guardians at home (Burke, Ayres, and Hagan-Burke, 2004).

Conclusions

There are two types of antisocial personality disorders including social pathology and sociopathology that are the consequence of interaction between genetic and environmental factors. Psychopaths do not decide on impulse; they normally plan out their schemes. They are more violent and aggressive Social paths commit crimes taking high risks and do not plan. They will leave clues to the crime they committed and are easily caught. Comorbidities for antisocial personality disorder include suicidal ideation, nicotine dependence, alcohol and drug abuse, and anxiety. ADHD, schizophrenia, and bipolar disorders are prevalent comorbid disorders in individuals who have both psychopathologic and social pathological disorders. Studies have shown that cognitive behavior therapy (CBT) and contingency management are effective treatments to control antisocial personality disorder. In general, pharmaceutical treatments are not effective in controlling antisocial personality disorder. Positive Behavior Support (PBS) has been initiated in many schools and have proven effective in reducing inappropriate and violent behaviors exhibited by students with antisocial personality disorder.

Recommendations

Interacting with students with sociopathic and psychopathic behaviors is disruptive, counter-productive, and at times dangerous. Educators, school administrators, therapists, and family members must be made aware of antisocial personality disorder. They must understand evidence-based practices based on scientific proof what strategies and intervention work best for the students. Constant professional development and training is needed to prepare those who interact with students with antisocial personality disorder. Educators, school administrators, and therapists must be prepared to keep all students, other adults including paraprofessionals, and other educators safe from aggressive and violent behaviors in all school settings.

Chapter 18
Social Skills Deficit and Speech/Language Disorders

Introduction

Social Skills Deficits and Speech/Language Disorders are two different mental conditions that have a lot in common. For this reason, these conditions have been combined in this chapter. Without typical social skill development, speech/language development will be hindered. Without speech/language development, social skills will show a deficit in development. Many times, in school settings, speech language therapist and social workers will combine their therapy sessions into one session because many of the interventions and evidence-based practices are the same used for both mental conditions. This chapter will explore social skills deficit, speech/language disorders, characteristics and traits, comorbid disorders, treatment, medications, and teaching students with these two conditions.

What is a Social Skills Deficit?

Social skills deficit is a defining characteristic of individuals diagnosed with ASD and other pervasive developmental disorders (PDD), which can hinder social functioning and put the individual at higher risk for developing inappropriate behavior, including self-injury and aggression. In social situations, when a student is unable to cooperate with others in a group, take turns, show empathy, is unable to listen to what others say, and understand and use non-verbal communication such as gesturing or body language, the student has social skills deficits. Social skills are required to interact and communicate with others daily. These skills can be practiced when interacting with others after observing and listening to them. The cause of social skills deficit can be genetic or environmental. Disruption in specific chromosomal arrangement leads to genetic dysfunctions and development in several parts of the brain. Comorbid developmental disorders such as ASD hinder social skills development (Chelly et al., 2006). Environmental factors include stressful conditions at home, daily living skills, and language development. Social skills will improve the more students are with other people. Understanding speech and language is required to develop social skills.

What is a Speech/Language Disorder?

A speech disorder is a condition when an individual is challenged in creating or forming sounds required to communicate with others. Others may find it difficult to understand a person with a speech disorder. A language disorder can cause challenges in the understanding or use of spoken, written, and other forms of language. Individuals with a language disorder may struggle with the form, content, or function of language including challenges involving grammar (syntax and/or morphology), semantics (meaning), or other aspects of language such as pragmatic language that is required for the social use of language. Causes of speech/language disorder can be either genetic, environmental, or both. According to a study of Varnes et al. (2006), mutation in the $FOXP_2$ gene cause pervasive communication disorders including a wide range of both expressive and receptive language.

Environmental causes of speech/language disorder include isolation from normal language development and lack of knowledge of the English language. Students who are English language learners exhibit some of the same deficits as individuals with genetic language disorders. Many times, students learning English as a second language have been misdiagnosed as a genetic disorder. In this case, English learned as a second language is environmental and the condition for typical learners in temporary until speaking English is mastered.

Characteristics/Traits

Students who have been diagnosed with a social skill deficit may be challenged asking precise and succinct questions. Lack of the ability to ask a question produces obstacles acquiring information and beginning a conversation. Students challenged with asking questions will seem withdrawn or disinterested and become anti-social. Students who exhibit social skill deficits have basic communication skill deficits. They fail to listen when others are speaking, have limited or no eye contact with others, lack of gesturing or body language skills, often speak out of turn. These students show lack of empathy toward others, show no feelings for their peers, and do not connect with other people. Their interpersonal skills are limited and do not like to share, join group activities, and are bad at taking turns. Problem solving skills are deficient when students do not or cannot ask for help, accept consequences, and apologize. Students may not feel accountable for their actions and will not accept blame or constructive criticism.

Students with speech/language disorder will use words improperly and will not understand the meanings of words. They are challenged expressing themselves verbally or in writing. They speak and write manifesting many errors in grammar. These students lack colloquial and academic vocabulary. They do not follow instructions because they have not understood them.

Comorbid Disabilities/Disorders

Comorbid disorders associated with both social skill deficit and speech/language disorder are ADHD, ASD, ODD, PDD, and SIB. Students with both ADHD and ASD exhibit speech/language disorder and social skills deficits. Speech/language disorder occurs in lower-functioning students with ASD. These same students will have lower levels of social interactions with their peers. Higher functioning students with ASD will have social skill deficits and possibly less speech/language challenges (Williams, Botting, and Boucher, 2008). Traumatized students with social skill disorders and speech/language deficits manifest different levels of ODD.

These conditions in students may be exacerbated by trauma caused by fetal alcohol syndrome (Henry, Sloane, and Black-Pond, 2007). Social skill deficits and speech/language disorder are comorbidities with PDD and SIB. What is challenging for educators is that every student is dissimilar. Some students will have different levels of these conditions, and others may not have one or more of these conditions at all. The prefrontal cortex region of the brain that controls executive functions is responsible for social skill development in individuals. The Broca area located in the left hemisphere and Wernicke area located in the superior temporal lobe regions of the brain control speech and language development. See Section I of the Appendix for approximate locations in the brain. Both social skill deficit and speech/language disorder are genetical conditions that are not curable, albeit treatable.

Treatments

The leading treatment for students with social skill deficit and speech/language disorder is therapy. School social workers are involved is setting up therapy sessions for one or a group of students. Speech/language pathologist hold therapy sessions for one or groups of students as well. These therapists will determine the appropriate sessions of students depending on the degree of severity of their conditions. Occasionally, therapy sessions for social skills development and speech/language may be held simultaneously or separately. This approach is widely accepted and affective (Edwards et al., 2015).

Medications

There has been little research on the use of drugs to treat students with social skill deficits and speech/language disorders. The use of drugs such as dexfenfluramine, naloxone, or secretin are not effective for these conditions. Risperidone when used to treat underlying conditions of ASD such as irritability has shown an improvement in some aspects of social skills of some students (Posey, Erickson, and McDougle, 2008). See Section II of the Appendix for List of Drugs with explanations of how they are used for treatment. In most cases, pharmaceutical approaches are used to only treat comorbidities of social skill deficits and speech/language disorders. There are no known medications that are effectively able to change the way someone interacts with others. Most medications used are for treating comorbidities of social skills deficit and speech/language disorder.

Teaching Students with Social Skills Deficit and Speech/Language Disorder

Teaching students with social skills deficit and speech/language disorder can be challenging. Educators will find increased challenges teaching math, reading, writing, and socialization skills of students in the classroom. These students are unable to meet the goals of socialization and speech/language. Not meeting these goals will hinder academic and social development. Over time, the lack of academic and social development will lead to inappropriate behavior such as PDD, ODD, and SIB if there are not therapeutical interventions in place (McLaughlin, 2011). Evidence-based practices should be in use in classroom. UDL and UbD have proven effective in teaching students with many disorders and disabilities. Repetition, use of video, pictures, modeling, scaffolding, and a lot of patience and understanding on the part of the educator have met with considerable success in the academic and social development of these students.

Conclusions

Social skill deficit is when individuals are unable to interact socially. They cannot join in other conversations, participate in group activities, know when to take turns, and gesture. This hinders social functioning. Speech/language disorder is a condition when individuals are challenged creating or forming sounds required to communicate with others. Often, pragmatic language is impaired. Social skill deficit and speech language disorder are caused by genetic, environmental, or both depending on different situations of the individual. Comorbid disorders associated with both social skill deficit and speech/language disorder are ADHD, ASD, ODD, PDD, and SIB. The leading treatment for students with social skill deficit and speech/language disorder is therapy. Evidence-based practices should be in use in classroom. UDL and UbD have proven effective in teaching students with many disorders and disabilities. Socialization with other individuals help in language development; however, sufficient communication skills are required to socialize. Because of this, social workers and speech/language pathologists may combine their therapy sessions. This practice is widely accepted and affective when there is collaboration with treatment methods between the social worker and speech language pathologist (Edwards et al., 2015).

Recommendations

The presence of students in school classrooms with social skill deficits and speech/language disorders is very common. Educators should be cross-trained to continue interventions and best practices that were initiated during the therapy sessions. Educators must understand the difference between a speech/language disorder and lack of knowledge of English. A speech/language disorder is caused by genetical mutations or environmental conditions. A typical student with lack of understanding of the English language is different because the student speaks another language other than

English as the first language. Both conditions may hinder social skills development.

Professional development and training will lead to better classroom management, better teaching methods, and enhanced student progress. Use of evidence-based practices based on empirical studies has proven successful. It is important that educators are patient with their students and are prepared to repeat as many times as necessary for the students to fully understand a concept.

Chapter 19
Tourette's Syndrome

Introduction

Tourette's Syndrome is a nervous system disorder including individuals who exhibit repetitive movements or unwanted sounds. The scope of this chapter will explore what Tourette's disorder is, its characteristics and traits, comorbidities, treatments, and medications to control this disorder, and how to teach students in the classroom with Tourette's. It is less common in the classroom, but it is easily identified when a student manifests the characteristics of this disorder.

What is Tourette's Syndrome?

Tourette's Syndrome (TS) is a neurodevelopmental disorder. It is part of a spectrum of tic disorders that becomes apparent in early childhood or adolescence. Current estimates indicate that one in 160 children from 5 to 17 in the United States has TS. There is no cure for TS, but because of dedicated research there are treatment options available. Some tic disorders are transient, but many will remain throughout life. In the last few decades, more people have been diagnosed with TS and it is becoming more common. Symptoms of TS can affect all areas of an individual's life. Preschool students through elderly individuals can exhibit symptoms of TS. Males are diagnosed three to four times more than females. All ethnic groups can have TS.

In lieu of extensive research over the last 40 years, there is still no clear understanding as to what causes TS. Research has centered on genetics. Attempts to isolate genes to provide advanced treatment have not been successful.

Characteristics/Traits

Individuals with TS exhibit involuntary muscle and vocal movements, called tics. These movements can be repetitive. Simple tic movements include blinking, neck jerks, sniffing, and shoulder shrugs. Complex tic movements involve multiple muscle groups including jumping, touching objects, or twirling. Movements can be gentle and forceful, enough to knock someone off a chair. Vocal tics can go from barely noticeable to very disruptive. These include barking, coughing, humming, screaming, shouting, making clicking noises while talking, screaming, and swearing. Individuals with TS can exhibit self-injurious behavior like playing with sharp objects, touching hot objects, and slapping oneself. These behaviors will vary with the degree of the disorder. In a school classroom, other students may hear and see these behaviors causing them to laugh. The student with TS will become annoyed and/or become sad and can influence inappropriate his behavior (Vahl, Jakubovski, and Müller-Vahl, 2016).

Comorbid Disabilities/Disorders

It is common for individuals with Tourette Syndrome (TS) to have comorbid disorders as well. These include ADHD, OCD, ODD, and ASD. The symptoms of TS may be more strongly related to OCD than ASD even though the repetitive behaviors of TS resemble the repetitive behaviors of ASD. Both ASD and TS are considered neurodevelopmental disorders. According to a study of Canitano and Vivanti (2007), there was an overlap between TD and repetitive movements and behaviors manifested by individuals with ASD and TD. The cognitive level and the degree of tics of the individual with ASD and TD are related. It was determined that tics prevalent in individuals with ASD should not be ignored and should be evaluated.

It is important to understand what parts of the brain TS affects. Computer Tomography (CT-scans) provide more detailed information of the brain. CT scans made indicated more gray matter in the thalamus, hypothalamus, and the midbrain than individuals without TS. The basal ganglia are also affected that help control body movements. See Section I. of the Appendix for approximate locations in the brain.

Treatments

Comprehensive Behavioral Intervention is a common method used to mitigate tic severity of TS. This method utilizes habit reversal therapy, behavior replace strategies, and learning to recognize anxiety, emotions, and phobias that are known to exacerbate tic severity. Early learning theories indicated that tics were learned and afterward could be unlearned. Current behavioral models show that tics are caused by functional and structural neurobiological abnormalities. However, current behavioral models maintain that despite the tics being of a biological origin, habit reversal therapy used in comprehensive behavioral intervention (CBIT) has shown that tic severity can be mitigated by using consequence variables such as social reactions, tangible reinforcers, and extrinsic rewards. Several studies using different methods have indicated that the habit reversal approach can treat tics effectively (Himle et al., 2006). Approaches using psychotherapy and drugs are also used.

Medications

Scientists suggest that an abnormal metabolism of the neurotransmitter dopamine and/or serotonin may be responsible of TS. This has resulted in better-quality tic control; however, the drugs for Tourette Syndrome used in the past and now are strong. Often, these drugs are untested in children, and have severe side effects (Himle et al., 2006).

Psychotic drugs used to mitigate the severity of tics include Fluphenazine, haloperidol (Haldol), risperidone (Risperdal)
and pimozide (Orap). As suggested, side effects experienced are weight gain and spontaneous repetitive movements. Tetrabenazine (Xenazine) does not cause these side effects, but it can cause severe depression. See Section II of the Appendix for List of Drugs with explanations of how they are used for treatment.

Teaching Students with Tourette's Syndrome

Teaching students with TS can be daunting for the educators, other students in the classroom, and the individual with TS. Other students may find the tics amusing and may laugh at the student. This action escalates inappropriate behavior and causes challenging classroom management. To minimize classroom disruption and help the student with TS, the following strategies and interventions are helpful. Explain to other students about the characteristics of TS and that the student is not deliberately exhibiting these tics and strange noises. Provide a separate location for testing with time limits waived. When the student experiences anxiety, provide a safe place.

Talk about possible solutions for reducing inappropriate tics with the student. Explain that spitting, swearing, and touching are considered inappropriate are not considered socially acceptable behavior. Work with the student to create another acceptable behavior to replace the inacceptable behavior. IEP team members should consider creating a behavior intervention plan (BIT). Comprehensive Behavioral Intervention for Tics (CBIT) have proven successful for many students with TS. There are other types of therapies available. Discuss these options with the school psychologist or social worker. For instruction, use evidence-based practices for best results.

Conclusions

Tourette's Syndrome (TS) is a nervous system disorder including individuals who exhibit repetitive movements or unwanted sounds and is a neurodevelopmental disorder. These actions are involuntary and are called tics. The most common comorbid disorders with TS include ADHD, OCD, ODD, and ASD. Comprehensive Behavioral Intervention (CBIT) is a common method used to mitigate tic severity of TS. Psychotic drugs are used to mitigate the severity of tics. Both therapy and drugs are used simultaneously or separately, depending on the individual with TS. Teaching students with TS can be challenging. With the use of appropriate strategies, interventions, and evidence-based practices, these challenges can be mitigated.

Recommendations

As more students are being diagnosed with TS, more of these students are entering into school classrooms. Many educators are not prepared to meet the challenges teaching these students. Both novice and experienced educator must be trained to understand TS and be aware of the characteristics of this disorder. Professional development and training will lead to better classroom management, better teaching methods, and enhanced student progress. Evidence-based practices should be employed for interventions, strategies, and instructional methods. On-going discussion with IEP team members to create a CBIT that is appropriate for the student with TS is essential for the academic and behavioral progress of the student.

Summary

Many educators are not prepared to confront the demands of special needs students with different disabilities and disorders. Teacher certification coursework often does not go deeply into student disabilities and disorder. Lack of professional preparation can be disastrous for classroom management and progress of atypical students. There are many psychological disorders that were not mentioned in this book. The intent of this book was to go more profoundly into more common classroom disorders. As you read through the previous chapters, you will find that many of the evidence-based practices are the same or similar among the different mental disorders. Many of the comorbid disorders are similar.

Treatments may be based on applied behavior analysis or therapy and medications differ depending on the mental disorder. Many of the same drugs are prescribed to treat the same psychological disorder as well as different medical conditions. Individuals may exhibit side effects common with prescription drugs in different ways or not at all. The degree the drugs help different individuals may vary. These psychotic drugs include antianxiety medication, antidepressants, antipsychotics, mood stabilizers, and stimulants. Educators may not be involved with the treatment and medications prescribed to students with different disorders but their awareness is important. Keeping abreast to the on-going treatments will help educators design appropriate classroom interventions. Being aware of the type of medications prescribed by health professionals will help the educator understand why the student is frequently sleeping in class or overactive.

Being familiar with the side effects of these drugs is very important as side effects will affect the academic progress and social development of the student. It is anticipated that after reading and becoming familiar with the contents of this book, educators and others who interact with typical and atypical students will be more aware and in a better position to confront student behaviors and avoid inappropriate classroom situations. Moreover, for information not included in these chapters, professionals should continue to expand their knowledge by continuing to read empirical studies and make changes when improved strategies and treatment occur over time.

Glossary

Accommodation: Educators provide changes to how a student learns classroom material by allowing the student to achieve the same tasks as their non-LD peers but with some variation in time, format, setting, and/or presentation.

Amygdala: Part of the limbic system of the brain the processes emotional events.

Anterior Cingulate Cortices: The region of the brain that controls complex cognitive functions; including empathy, impulse control, emotion, and decision-making.

Antisocial Personality Disorder: Is a mental health disorder described as having disregard for other people such as empathy or feeling toward others.

Applied Behavior Analysis: Is a scientific procedure concerned with applying evidence-based approaches based upon the tenets of respondent and operant conditioning to change behavior of social significance.

Attention Deficit Hyperactivity Disorder (ADHD): Is a syndrome found in children and adults that manifests developmentally unsuitable inattention, impulsive behavior, and hyperactivity that exhibits behavioral impairments at home, school, or workplace.

Autism Spectrum Disorder (ASD): Refers to a broad range of neurodevelopmental disorders with characteristics of impaired speech-language, social skills deficits, occupational impairments, repetitive behaviors, interests, and activities.

Autonomic Nervous System: Is a control system that functions mainly unconsciously and regulates bodily functions, including the heart rate, digestion, respiratory rate, pupillary response, urination, and sexual arousal. This system also functions as the principal mechanism in control of the fight-or-flight response.

Basal Ganglia: The part of the brain that control body movements such as fine and gross motor movements.

Behavior: Is how a person reacts to the environment that influences emotions, thoughts, and other internal mental processes causing overt manifestation of a certain response.

Behavior Educational Intervention (BEI): Training to enhance ability to promote appropriate behavior.

Bipolar Disorder: A manic-depressive brain condition that causes irregular mood-shifts to occur.

Broca's Region: Is an area in the brain in the frontal lobe of the dominant hemisphere, usually the left, with functions linked to speech production.

Catatonic: Is staying still without movement, immobile, lack of speech, unresponsive.

Cerebellum: Is the part of the brain responsible for organizing voluntary movements; including motor skills such as balance, coordination, and posture.

Cognitive Behavioral Rehabilitation: Applies different treatment approaches that are intended to address challenges with attention, judgment, learning, memory, perception, and planning.

Cognitive Behavioral Therapy (CBT): refers to types of psychotherapy that treat mental health disorders. CBT target inappropriate behaviors to replace these behaviors with appropriate behaviors.

Comorbid, Comorbidities: Is the presence of one or more additional mental disorders often co-occurring with a primary disorder.

Comprehensive Behavioral Intervention (CBIT): Is a common method used to mitigate tic severity of TS.

Congenital Blindness: Is a disease usually occurring during early adolescence that if left untreated may lead to permanent blindness.

Contingency Management: Is a behavior modification technique that reinforces desired behaviors through extrinsic rewards.

Corpus Callosum: Is a collection of nerve fibers in the longitudinal fissure of the brain that allows corresponding areas of the left and right cerebral hemispheres to communicate.

Cortical Thinning: Is the loss of gray matter in the cortical region of the brain and has been suggested to be a reliable marker of brain atrophy. This can lead to many brain disorders.

Delusion: Eccentric beliefs or feelings that are disputed by reality or rational argument. This is a common condition manifested by individuals with schizophrenia.

Diagnostic and Statistical Manual of Mental Disorders (DSM-5): Is the handbook used by health care professionals in the United States and abroad as the authoritative guide to the diagnosis of mental disorders. DSM-5 refers to the edition of the handbook.

Disability: Is a condition of the body or mind that makes it more challenging for the person with the condition to do certain activities and interact with others around them.

Disorder: Is a behavioral or mental pattern that is a causation of significant distress or abnormal thoughts, feeling, or behaviors.

Down's Syndrome: Is a condition in which a child is born with an extra copy of their 21st chromosome that can cause mental and physical developmental delays.

Dyscalculia: Is a disorder when individuals exhibit difficulties with math, including weaknesses in number sense, and challenges applying mathematical principles to solve problems.

Dyslexia: Is a disorder that individuals have when learning to read or interpret words, letters, and other symbols.

Echolalia: Is a congenial disorder characterized by the repetition of spoken words. Students with Echolalia are challenged conveying their thoughts.

Electroconvulsive Therapy (ECT): Is given to a patient under general anesthesia when small amounts of electrical current are passed through the brain.

Emotional Disability: Is a psychopathological disorder that manifests calamity associated with emotional and mental illnesses. This disability influences a person's ability to effectively recognize, interpret, control, and express fundamental emotions.

Evidence-Based Practices: Is applying scientifically proven methods based on peer-reviewed empirical research. These practices are applied when using interventions and strategies in the classroom.

Executive Function Disorder: Is a range of cognitive, behavioral, and emotional constraints that often occur because of another mental disorder or a traumatic brain injury.

Exposure Response Therapy: Is a therapy that suggests individuals to face their fears and allow obsessive thoughts to occur without neutralizing them with other urges or needs.

Fetal Alcohol Syndrome (FASD): Is prevalent syndrome manifested by students when their biological mothers indulged in the excessive use of alcohol during pregnancy.

Fine Motor Skills: Is the ability to make movements using the small muscles in our hands, fingers, and wrists.

Fragile X Syndrome: Is a genetic disorder that is caused by changes in a gene that scientists call the FMR1 gene. This is when the FMR1 does not produce a protein called Fragile X that is necessary for typical brain development. Lack of this protein causes Intellectual Disability.

Frontal Lobe: Each of the paired lobes of the brain is located behind the forehead, including areas concerned with behavior, learning, personality, and voluntary movement.

Ganglion Cells: Are the projection nerve cells of the vertebrate retina, that transmit information from other retinal nerve cells to other areas of the brain.

Gastroesophageal Reflux: Known as GERD that occurs when stomach acid frequently flows back into the tube connecting your mouth and stomach.

Gastrointestinal: This term relates to both stomach and the intestines.

Genetic: This refers to genes or heredity. Individuals inherit medical and mental conditions from parents through our DNA.

Gross Motor Skill: Is muscle development that permits us to stand up, walk and run, and walk upstairs.

Group Psychotherapy: Is a form of therapy consisting of two or more individuals that meet under the guidance of a professionally trained therapist to help themselves and one another.

Hallucinations: When individuals perceive they see an object, person, or thing that is not present.

Hippocampus: Is a dense brain structure that is located deep within temporal lobe. The major purpose is processing what is learned and memory.

Hyperosmia: Is a sensory disorder that is the cause of an increased olfactory acuity. This is an increased sense of smell induced by sensitivity to chemicals.

Hyperprolactinemia: This is an over-production of prolactin, a hormone controlling milk production in mammals. This condition can be induced because of a side effect of Risperidone or Risperdal.

Individualized Education Plan (IEP): Is a plan created to ensure that a student who has a disability or disorder identified under the Disabilities Education Act (IDEA) and is attending a private or public elementary or secondary school receives specialized instruction and related services.

Inferior Left Temporal Lobe: Is part of the cortex of the brain that processes information for the visual recognition of objects.

Inhibitory Control: Manages the suppression of goal-irrelevant stimuli and behavioral responses. It gives a person the ability to resist interference from distracting stimuli. This is part of the executive function of the brain.

Intellectual Disability (ID): Is defined as limited abilities to learn, to solve problems, socialize, converse, and communicate, and function in day-to-day life.

Learning Disability (LD): Individuals with challenges in specific cognitive development and academic progress with otherwise typical levels of intellectual functioning are considered as having a learning disability.

Limbic System: Is the part of the brain involved in our behavioral and emotional responses, especially when it comes to behaviors needed for survival: feeding, reproduction and caring for the young, and fight or flight responses consisting of the amygdala, hippocampus, hypothalamus, and the thalamus.

Manic Depressive Brain Condition: Is part of bipolar disorder when the individual has increased activity in the amygdala and leads to aggression, depression, or anxiety.

Mental Contamination: Is the process when an individual has an undesired response because of mental processing that is unconscious or cannot be controlled.

Misophonia: Is an unpleasant response to different sounds made by objects or other individuals, like a ticking pendulum in a clock, clicking of a pen, sniffing, tapping, or any repetitive noise.

Modeling: Is when an educator demonstrates to students how to perform a skill, routine, or procedure, and shows them what to notice.

Multi-Disciplinary Evaluation Team (MET): Prior to receiving services under Special Education, a student must be referred, and participate in assessments and evaluation to determine if the student is eligible for Special Education. Usually, the team consists of a psychologist, speech/language pathologist, social worker, general education teacher, special education teacher, school district representative, the parents, and student. There may be other participants depending on the disability or disorder.

Multiple Intelligences: Is a theory that describes different ways individuals learn and acquire information. Multiple intelligences include the use of words, numbers, pictures, and music, social interactions, introspection, physical movement and understanding nature. Individuals may have more than one intelligence.

Neurobiological: Is the neural functioning of neurons and neurotransmitters that shape and influence the behavior of an individual.

Neurodevelopmental Disorders: The most common include ASD, ADHD, FAS, fragile X syndrome, and schizophrenia.

Obsessive Compulsive Disorder (OCD): Is an incapacitating cerebral disorder that involves stressful obsessions leading to repetitive compulsive behaviors.

Occipital Lobe: Is the visual processing part of the human brain containing most of the anatomical region of the visual cortex.

Occipital Cortex: The Occipital Lobe is part of the visual cortex that processes vision.

Olfactory Receptors: Detect air-borne odor molecules that enter the nose. These receptors are cell membranes in the nasal cavity.

Olfactory Sensory Nerve: Are neurons in the nasal epithelium that detect and send odor or sent information to the central nervous system.

Oppositional Defiant Disorder (ODD): Oppositional defiant disorder is a reoccurring pattern of developmentally unsuitable, pessimistic, defiant, and disobedient behavior toward authority figures.

Orbitofrontal Cortex: Is the area of the prefrontal cortex that sits just above the eye sockets. It processes along with the limbic system emotion and memory.

Paranoid: Is a feeling that a person is being threatened including other people watching you or acting against you, even though there is lack of proof that it is true.

Paraprofessional: This is a person that assists teachers in inclusive and self-contained classroom settings with the immediate needs and support of special-needs students. This person is also called a teacher's aide.

Parietal Gray Matter: Is neural tissue of the brain and spinal cord that contains nerve-cell bodies as well as nerve fibers. This gray matter processes information sent from the axons (white matter).

Pathogenesis: Is how a disease advances and the contiguous and linked events lead to the disease.

Pathogens: Are the bacteria, virus, or another microorganism that may cause a disease or illness.

Pervasive Developmental Disorder, Not Otherwise Specified (PDD-NOS): Is a group of disorders with compromised development of social skills, verbal and non-verbal communication/language, imaginative activity, and having few interests and activities that tend to be repetitive.

Pharmaceutical: Is related to drugs used for medical purposes, their sale and distribution.

Photophobia: Is a sensory disorder that is triggered by light that causes discomfort in the eye or head.

Photoreceptors: Is a sensory cell that reacts to light coming in to connect with it.

Placebos: Is a pill or medicine that has not active ingredients other than sugar or starch that is used for a psychological benefit. It is also known as a fake pill.

Post-Traumatic Stress Disorder (PTSD): Is a mental health disorder that is caused by a terrifying event including a traumatic brain injury, or an event that is experienced or witnessed by an individual.

Prefrontal Cortex: Is the region of the brain that makes up the frontal area of the frontal lobe. It processes information involving higher cognition thoughts, planning, personality, and appropriate social behavior.

Psychiatric Disorders: Are mental illness that greatly impact behavior, thinking, moods, and significantly increase the probability of disability, pain, death, or loss of freedom.

Psychological Counseling: Addresses family, school, social deficits, and the work environment, including family members in the therapy.

Psychopathic Conditions: Is a mental antisocial behavior that includes lack of friendship and empathy and having a tendency toward extreme egocentric behaviors.

Psychopathology: An individual who is a psychopathological characteristic is thought to have acquired the disorder through genetic heredity. Colloquially, these individuals are called psychopaths. Psychopaths tend to be more manipulative, can be seen by others as more charismatic, charming, appear to lead a normal life, and minimize their risk of being caught in criminal activities. It is considered an antisocial personality disorder.

Psychotherapy: Involves a psychologist or therapist who leads one or more individuals with a mental disorder. Sessions meet for an hour or two every week. No drugs are used in psychotherapy

Psychotic Disorders: Are severe mental conditions that cause irregular reasoning and perceptions.

Repetitive Behaviors: Are irregular actions that include repetitionrigidity, inappropriate atypical behaviors such as pacing, hand flapping, or verbal repletion. These behaviors are common comorbidities with neurodevelopmental disorders, especially ASD.

Rett Syndrome: Is a neurodevelopmental disorder that is considered as ASD. Both Rett Syndrome and ASD are neurodevelopmental disorders. It is categorized as an autism spectrum disorder, but, unlike most forms of autism, Rett Syndrome is different because the cause is due to a mutation in a protein known as MeCP2.

Scaffolding: Is analyzing and breaking up the learning into chunks or pieces and providing a tool, or structure, with each chunk to bring the chunks together and synthesize the learning.

Schizophrenia: Is a pervasive developmental disorder. Schizophrenia is a grave mental illness characterized by disjointed or irrational thoughts, inexplicable behavior and speech, and delusions or hallucinations, such as hearing voices or thinking someone will do harm.

Self-Injurious Behavior (SIB): Is a behavior in which an individual harms (or attempts to harm) oneself intentionally and physically.

Sensory Disorders: Sensory disorder is caused by over-stimuli of the senses including hyperosmia, misophonia, photophobia, and tactile dysfunction.

Social Pathology: An individual who is considered to have a social pathological disorder who manifests antisocial behavior that is caused by a way of believing, home environment, and/or brain injury. Commonly, these individuals are known as social paths. It is considered an antisocial personality disorder.

Social Skill Deficit: Individuals who exhibit social skill deficits have basic communication skill deficits. They fail to listen when others are speaking, have limited or no eye contact with others, lack of gesturing or body language skills, often speak out of turn.

Somatosensory Center: This area of the cortex in the human brain is in the postcentral gyrus of the parietal lobe. This is the principal sensory receptive area for the sense of touch.

Speech/Language Disorder: Individuals with speech/language disorder will use words improperly and will not understand the meanings of words. They are challenged expressing themselves verbally or in writing. They speak and write manifesting many errors in grammar. These individuals lack colloquial and academic vocabulary. They do not follow instructions because they are not understood.

Superior Temporal Lobe Region: This includes a region of the brain where auditory signals from the cochlea arrive at the cerebral cortex and are processed by the primary auditory cortex in the left temporal lobe.

Tactile Dysfunction: Is a type of sensory dysfunction that causes the sense of touch to be over-stimulated to the point of discomfort or even pain.

Thalamus: Is a small formation within the brain in the region above the brain stem between the cerebral cortex and the midbrain. It has substantial neuro connections to both. The principal function of the thalamus is to transmit motor and sensory signals to the cerebral cortex.

Therapy: Is a treatment intended to control, relieve, or heal a disorder without the use of drugs.

Tourette's Syndrome (TS): Is a neurodevelopmental disorder. It is part of a spectrum of tic disorders that becomes apparent in early childhood or adolescence. Individuals with TS exhibit repetitive movements or unwanted sounds.

Transcortical Sensory Aphasia (TSA): is a type of aphasia involving damage to areas of the temporal lobe of the brain. This damage results in symptoms including fluent speech with semantic paraphasia present, poor auditory comprehension, and relatively intact repetition.

Treatment and Education of Autistic and Communication-Handicapped Children (TEACCH): This is a post-secondary intervention program developed to support the transition to employment and post-secondary education for 16–21-year-olds with Autism Spectrum Disorder (ASD).

Understanding by Design (UbD): Understanding by Design (UbD) emphasizes goals and how and what should be learned while using a backward approach to achieve those goals.

Universal Design for Learning (UDL): Focuses on the learning needs of students as a top priority. UDL uses the process of developing flexible learning environments and learning spaces that can accommodate individual learning differences for typical and atypical learners.

Wernicke Area: This region of the brain contains motor neurons involved in the comprehension of speech. This area is in the posterior third of the upper temporal convolution of the left hemisphere of the brain.

References

American Psychiatric Association. (2013). *Diagnostic and Statistical Manual of Mental Disorders* (*DSM-5*). Washington, D.C.: American Psychiatric Publishing.

American Psychological Association. (2020). *What Is Cognitive Behavioral Therapy?* Washington, D.C.: APA Publishing. Retrieved January 19, 2021 from: https://www.apa.org/pub

Angelka, K., and Goran, A. (2018). Learning problems in children with mild intellectual disability. *International Journal of Cognitive Research in Science, Engineering, and Education, 6*(1), 31–37.

Angermeyer, M. C., and Hatschinger, H. (1996). Relatives' beliefs about the causes of schizophrenia. *Acta Psychiatrica Scandinavica, 93*(3), 199–204.

Arzeno Ferrao, Y., Almeida, V. P., Bedin, N. R., Rosa, R., D'Arrigo Busnello, E. (2006). Impulsivity and compulsivity in patients with trichotillomania or skin picking compared with patients with obsessive-compulsive disorder. *Comprehensive Psychiatry, 47*(4), 282–288.

Azeredo, A., Moreira, D., and Barbosa, F. (2018). ADHD, CD, and ODD: Systematic review of genetic and environmental risk factors. *Research in Developmental Disabilities, 82.* 10–19.

Bauer, M., and Pfennig, A. (2005). Epidemiology of bipolar disorders. *Epilepsia, 46*(4), 8–13.

Baron-Cohen, S., and Belmonte, M. K. (2005), Autism: A window onto the development of the social and the analytic brain. *Annual Review of Neuroscience, 28*, 109–126.

Boatman, D., Gordon, B., Hart, J., Selnes, O., Miglioretti, D., and Lenz, F. (2000). Transcortical sensory aphasia: revisited and revised. *Brain, (123)*8, 1634–1642.

Briars, L., and Todd, T. (2016). A review of pharmacological management of attention-deficit/hyperactivity disorder. The *Journal of Pediatric Pharmacology and Therapeutics: JPPT: The Official Journal of PPAG, 21*(3), 192–206.

Brown, T. E. (2009). *ADHD Comorbidities: Handbook for ADHD Complications in Children and Adults* (ed.). Arlington, VA: American Psychiatric Publishing Inc.

Buoli, M., Serati, M., Caldiroli, A., Cremaschi, L., and Altamura, A. C. (2017). Neurodevelopmental versus neurodegenerative model of schizophrenia and bipolar disorder: Comparison with physiological brain development and aging. *Psychiatria Danubina, 29*(1), 24–27.

Burke, M. D., Ayres, K., and Hagan-Burke, S. (2004). Preventing school-based antisocial behaviors with school-wide positive behavioral support. *Journal of Early and Intensive Behavior Intervention, 1*(1), 65–73.

Büttner, G., and Hasselhorn, M. (2011). Learning Disabilities: Debates on definitions, causes, subtypes, and responses. *International Journal of Disability, Development and Education, 58*(1), 75–87.

Canitano, R., and Vivanti, G. (2007). Tics and Tourette syndrome in autism spectrum disorders. *Autism, The International Journal of Research and Practice, 11*(1), 19–28.

Carter, J. C., Lanham, D. C., Pham, D., Bibat, G., Naidu, S., and Kaufmann, W. E. (2008). Selective cerebral volume reduction in Rett syndrome: A multiple approach MRI study. *American Journal of Neuroradiology, 29*(3), 436–441.

Cartreine, J. (2019). Misophonia: When sounds really do make you "crazy". *Harvard Health Blog.* Retrieved on February 8, 2021 from: https://www.health.harvard.edu/blog/misophonia-sounds-really-make-crazy-2017042111534

Chapleau, C. A., Lane, J., Pozzo-Miller, L., and Percy, A. K. (2013). Evaluation of current pharmacological treatment options in the management of Rett syndrome: From the present to future therapeutic alternatives. *Current Clinical Pharmacology, 8*(4), 358–369.

Charlop-Christy, M. H., and Kelso, S. E. (2003). Teaching children with autism conversational speech using cue card/written script program. *Education and Treatment of Children, 26*(2), 108–127.

Chelly, J., Khelfaoui, M., Francis, F., Chérif, B., and Bienvenu, T. (2006). Genetics and pathophysiology of mental retardation. *European Journal of Human Genetics, 14*, 701–713.

Cortese S., Sun S., Zhang, J., Sharma E., Chang, Z., Kuja-Halkola, R., Almqvist, C., Larsson, H., and Faraone, S. V. (2018). Association between attention-deficit/hyperactivity disorder and asthma: a systematic review and meta-analysis and a Swedish population-based study. *Lancet Psychiatry, 5*(9), 717–726.

Conterio, K., Lader, W., and Bloom, J. K. (1998). Bodily harm: The breakthrough treatment program for self-injurers. New York: Hyperion.

Crowell, S. E., Beauchaine, T. P., McCauley, E., Smith, C. J., Stevens, A. L., Sylvers, P. (2005). Psychological, autonomic, and serotonergic correlates of parasuicide among adolescent girls. *Development and Psychopathology, 17*, 1105–27.

Del Casale, A. et al. (2020). Multiple chemical sensitivity syndrome: A principal component analysis of symptoms. *International Journal of Environmental Research and Public Health, (17)*18, 1–12.

Dillon, G. V., Underwood, J. D., and Freemantle, L. J. (2016). Autism and the U.K. secondary school experience. *Focus of Autism and Other Developmental Disabilities, 31*(3), 220–229.

Dittrick, K. et al. (2020). Alterations of empathy in mothers with a history of early life maltreatment, depression, and borderline personality disorder and their effects on child psychopathology. *Psychological Medicine, 50*(7), 1182–1190.

Durston, S. (2010). Imaging genetics in ADHD, *NeuroImage, 53*(3), 832–838.

Edwards, C. M., Newell, J. M., Rich, D. W., and Hitchcock, L. I. (2015). Teaching interprofessional practice: An exploratory course assignment in social work and speech language pathology. *Journal of Teaching in Social Work, 35*(5), 529–543.

Erfanian, M., Kartsonaki, C., and Keshavarz, A. (2019). Misophonia and comorbid psychiatric symptoms: A preliminary study of clinical findings. *Nordic Journal of Psychiatry, 73*(4–5), 219–228.

Family Center for Recovery. (2021). *What Happens When You Baker Act Someone?* Retrieved from: What Happens When you Baker Act Someone? – Family Center for Recovery (fcfrmd.com).

Faraone, S.V., Asherson, P., Banaschewski, T., Biederman, J., Buitelaar, J. K., Ramos-Quiroga, J., A., Rohde, L., A., Sonuga-Barke, E. J. S., Tannock, R., and Franke, B. (2015). Attention-deficit/hyperactivity disorder. *Nat Rev Dis Primers 6*(1), 1–23.

Fard, R. F., Hosseini, M. R., Faraji, M., and Oskouei, A., O. (2018). Building characteristics and sick building syndrome among primary school students. *Sri Lanka Journal of Child Health, 47*(4), 332–337.

Frith, U., and Happé, F. (2005). Autism spectrum disorder. *Current Biology 15*(19), 786–790.

Goldstein, B. I., et al. (2017). The international society for bipolar disorders task force report on pediatric bipolar disorder: Knowledge to date and directions for future research. *Bipolar Disorders, 19*(7), 524–543.

Grandin, T. (1995). *Learning and Cognition in Autism* (ed.). Plenum Press, New York, NY: Plenum Press.

Gottfried, M. A., and Harven, A. (2014). The effect of having classmates with emotional and behavioral disorders and the protective nature of peer gender. *The Journal of Educational Research, 108*(1), 45–61.

Grossi, D., Marcone, R., Cinquegrana, T., and Gallucci, M. (2013). On the differential nature of induced and incidental echolalia in autism. *Journal of Intellectual Disability Research, 57*(10), 903–912.

Hamilton, S. S., and Armando, J. (2008). Oppositional deviant disorder. *American Family Physician, 78*(7), 861–866.

Han, P., Stiller-Stut, F. P., Fjaeldstad, A., and Hummel, T. (2020). Greater hippocampal gray matter volume in subjective hyperosmia: A voxel-based morphometry study. *Scientific Reports, 10*(18869), 1–10.

Henry, J., Sloane, M., and Black-Pond, C. (2007). Neurobiology and neurodevelopmental impact of childhood traumatic stress and prenatal alcohol exposure. *Language, Speech, and Hearing Services in Schools, 38*, 99–108.

Herscu, P. et al. (2020). The SOFIA study: negative multi-center study of low dose fluoxetine on repetitive behaviors in children and adolescents with autistic disorder. *Journal of Autism and Developmental Disorders, 50*(9), 3233–3244.

Hetzroni, O. E., and Tannous, J. (2004) Effects of a computer-based intervention program on the communicative functions of children with autism. *Journal of Autism and Developmental Disorders, 34*(2), 95–103.

Himle, M. B., Woods, D. W., Piacentini, J. C., and Walkup, J. T. (2006). Brief review of habit reversal training for Tourette Syndrome. *Journal of Child Neurology, 21*, 719–725.

Hunnikin, L. M., Wells, A. E., Ash, D. P., and Van Goozen, S. H. M. (2020). The nature and extent of emotion recognition and empathy impairments in children showing disruptive behavior referred into a criminal prevention programme. *European Child and Adolescent Psychiatry, 29*, 363–371.

Karlsgodt, K. H., Sun, D., and Cannon, T. D. (2010). Structural and functional brain abnormalities in schizophrenia. *Current Directions in Psychological Science, 19*(4), 226–231.

Karatzias, T., Gumley, A., Power, K., and O'Grady, M. (2007). Illness appraisals and self-esteem as correlates of anxiety and affective comorbid disorders in schizophrenia. *Comprehensive Psychiatry 48*(4), 371–375.

Khalifa, N. R., Gibbon S., Völlm, B. A., Cheung, N. H. Y., McCarthy L. (2020). The use of medication to treat people with antisocial personality disorder. *Cochrane Database of Systematic Reviews, 9*(3), 1–4.

Kiani, R., Blaumik, S., Tyrer, F., Bankart, J., Miller, H., Cooper, S. A., and Brugha, T. A. (2019). The relationship between symptoms of autism spectrum disorder and visual impairment among adults with intellectual disability. *Autism Research, 12*(9), 1411–1422.

King, B. H., Hollander, E., and Sikicki, L. (2009). Lack of efficacy of citalopram in children with autism spectrum disorders and high levels of repetitive behavior: Citalopram ineffective in children with autism. *Archives of General Psychiatry 66*(6), 583–590.

Knight, V., Sartini, E., and Spriggs, A. D. (2015). Evaluating visual activity schedules as evidence-based practice for individuals with autism spectrum disorders. *Journal of Autism and Developmental Disorders, 45*(1), 157–178.

Kouzis, A. C., and Eaton, W. W. (1994). Emotional disability days: Prevalence and predictors. *American Journal of Public Health 84*(4), 1304–1307.

Landerl, K., Fussenegger, B., Moll, K., and Willburger, E. (2009). Dyslexia and dyscalculia: Two learning disorders with different cognitive profiles. *Journal of Experimental Child Psychology, 103*, 309–324.

Leonard, H. et al. (2013). Assessment and management of nutrition and growth in Rett syndrome. *Journal of Pediatric Gastroenterology and Nutrition, 57*(4), 451–460.

Lobb, A. (2017). Critical empathy. *Constellations: An International Journal of Critical and Democratic Theory, 24*(4) 594–607.

Masi, G. et al. (2020). Suicidal ideation and suicidal attempts in referred adolescents with high functioning autism spectrum disorder and comorbid bipolar disorder: A pilot study. *Brain Sciences, 10*(10). 750.

Matthys, W., Vanderschuren, L. J., Schutter, D., J., and Lochman, J. E. (2012). Impaired neurocognitive functions affect social learning processes in oppositional defiant disorder and conduct disorder: Implications for interventions. *Clinical Family and Child Psychology, 15*, 234–246.

Matthys, W., and Schutter, D. J. (2021). Increasing effectiveness of cognitive behavioral therapy for conduct problems in children and adolescents: What can we learn from neuroimaging studies? *Clinical Child and Family Psychology Review, 24*(1), 1–16.

Mayo Clinic. (2021). *Fetal alcohol syndrome.* Retrieved January 21, 2021 from: https://www.mayoclinic.org

Mayo Clinic. (2021). *Learning disorders: Know the signs, how to help.* Retrieved February 6, 2021 from: https://www.mayoclinic.org/healthy-lifestyle/childrens-health/in-depth/learning-disorders/art-20046105

Mayo Clinic. (2021). *Obsessive Compulsive Disorder (OCD).* Retrieved February 14, 2021 from: https://www.mayoclinic.org/diseases-conditions/obsessive-compulsive-disorder/symptoms-causes/syc-20354432

Mayo Clinic. (2021). *Schizophrenia.* Retrieved March 4, 2021 from: https://www.mayoclinic.org/diseases-conditions/schizophrenia/diagnosis-treatment/drc-20354449

Mazza, M., Pino, M. C., Vagnetti, R., Filocamo, A., Attanasio, M., Calvarese, A., and Valenti, M. (2020). Intensive intervention for adolescents with autism spectrum disorder: Comparison of three rehabilitation treatments, *International Journal of Psychiatry in Clinical Practice, 24*(4), 1–9.

McLaughlin, M. R. (2011). Speech and language delay in children. *American Family Physician, 10,* 1183–1188.

Meier, S. M., Peterson, L., Schendel, D. E., Mattheisen, M., Mortensen, P. B., and Mors, O. (2015). Obsessive-compulsive disorder and autism spectrum disorders: Longitudinal and offspring risk. *PLoS One, 10*(11), 1–12.

Melina, R. (2011). Most teens grow out of self-harm behavior. *Life Science,* 1–3. Retrieved on March 8, 2021 from Most Teens Grow Out of Self-Harm Behavior | Live Science.

Minshawi, N. F., Hurwitz, S., Fodstad, J. C., Biebi, S., Morriss, D. H., and McDougle, C. J. (2014). The association between self-injurious behaviors and autism spectrum disorders. *Psychology Research and Behavior Management, 7,* 125–136.

Moran, P., and Hodgins, S. (2004). The correlates of comorbid antisocial personality disorder in schizophrenia. *Schizophrenia Bulletin, 30*(4), 791–802.

Mostafavi, M., and Gaitanis, J. (2020). Autism spectrum disorder and medical cannabis: Review and clinical experience. *Seminars in pediatric neurology, 35*(4), 1–5.

Muehlenkamp, J. J. (2005). Self-Injurious behavior as a separate clinical syndrome. *American Journal of Orthopsychiatry, 75*(2), 324–333.

Neul, J. L. (2012). The relationship of Rett syndrome and MECP2 disorders to Autism. *Dialogues in Clinical Neuroscience, 14*(3, 253–263.

Noordermeer, et al. (2017). Risk factors for comorbid oppositional defiant disorder in attention-deficit/hyperactivitydisorder. *European Child and Adolescent Psychiatry, 26*(10), 1155–1164.

Oliver, C., Licence, L., and Richards, C. (2017). Self-injurious behaviour in people with intellectual disability and autism spectrum disorder. *Current Opinion in Psychiatry, (30)* 2, 97–101.

Page, J., Lustenberger, C., and Fröhlich, F. (2020). Nonrapid eye movement sleep and risk for autism spectrum disorder in early development: A topographical electroencephalogram pilot study. *Brain and Behavior, 10*(3), 1–14.

Pallanti, S., Grassi, G., Sarrecchia, E. D., Cantisani, A., Pellegrini, M. (2011). Obsessive–compulsive disorder comorbidity: Clinical assessment and therapeutic implications. *Frontiers in Psychiatry, 2*(70), 1–11.

Parekh, R. (2017). What is intellectual Disability? *American Psychiatric Association.* Retrieved on February 2, 2021 from: https://www.psychiatry.org/patients-families/intellectual-disability/what-is-intellectual-disability.

Paulis, D. L., and Alsobrook, J. P. (1999). The inheritance of obsessive-compulsive disorder. *Child and Adolescent Psychiatric Clinics, 8*(3), 481–496.

Perkins, M. (1994). Repetitiveness in language disorders: A new analytical procedure. *Clinical linguistics and phonetics, 8*(4), 321–336.

Posey, D. J., Erickson, C. A., and McDougle, C. J. (2008). Developing drugs for core social and communication impairment in autism. *Child and Adolescent Psychiatric Clinics of North America, 17*(4), 787–801.

Potgieter, I., MacDonald, C., Partridge, L., Cima, R., Sheldrake, J., and Hoare, D. J. (2019). Misophonia: A scoping review of research. *Clinical Psychology, 75*(7), 1203–1208.

Rappley, M. D. (2005). Attention deficit–hyperactivity disorder. *The New England Journal of Medicine, 352*(2), 165–173.

Reddihough, D.S., Marraffa, C., Mouti, A., O'Sullivan, M., Lee, K. J., Orsini, F., Hazell, P., Granich, J., Whitehouse, A. J. O., Wray, J., Dossetor, D., Santosh, P., Silove, N., and Kohn, M. (2019). Effect of fluoxetine on obsessive-compulsive behaviors in children and adolescents with autism spectrum disorders: A randomized clinical trial. *JAMA 322*(16), 1561–1569.

Rogers, J. C., and De Brito, S. A. (2015). Cortical and subcortical gray matter volume in youths with conduct problems: A meta-analysis. *JAMA Psychiatry, 73*(1), 64–72.

Ross, R. G., Heinlein, S., and Tregellas, H. (2006). High rates of comorbidity are found in childhood-onset schizophrenia. *Schizophrenia Research, 88*(1–3), 90–95.

Schalock, R. L., Luckasson, R., Tassé, M. J., and Verdugo, M. A. (2018). A holistic theoretical approach to intellectual disability: Going beyond the four current perspectives. *Intellectual and Developmental Disabilities, 56*(2), 79–89.

Selekman, M. D. (2010). Helping self-harming students. *Educational Leadership, 67*(4), 48–53.

Şener, S., and Çokçalışkan, A. (2018). An investigation between multiple intelligences and learning styles. *Journal of Education and Training Studies, 6*(2), 125–132.

Şener, S., and Kilic, B. G. (2005). Family functioning and psychosocial characteristics in children with attention deficit hyperactivity disorder with comorbid oppositional defiant disorder or conduct disorder. *Turkish Journal of Psychiatry, 16*(1), 1–7.

Simonoff, et al. (2008). Psychiatric disorders in children with autism spectrum disorders: Prevalence, comorbidity, and associated factors in a population-derived sample. *Journal of American Academy of Child and Adolescent Psychiatry, 47*(8), 921–929.

Smith, B. D. (2005). Self-mutilation and pharmacotherapy. *Psychiatry, 2*(10), 28–37.

Son, Y., Kim, S., and Lee, J. (2021). Self-Injurious behavior in community youth. *International Journal of Environmental and Public Health, 18*(1), 1–16.

Stiegler, L. N. (2015). Examining the Echolalia Literature: Where Do Speech-Language Pathologists Stand? *American Journal of Speech-Language Pathology, 24*(4), 750–762.

Stone, J. A., and Sias, S. M. (2003). A bi-modal treatment approach to working with adolescent females. Journal of Mental Health Counseling, 25, 112–125.

Swanson, J. M., Volkow, N. D., Newcorn, J., Casey, B. J., Moyzis, R., Grandy D., and Posner, M. (2006). *Encyclopedia of cognitive science* (ed.). Hoboken NJ: John Wiley and Sons, Ltd.

Swartz, H. A. et al. (2018). Psychotherapy alone and combined with medication as treatments for bipolar II depression: A randomized controlled trial. *Journal of Clinical Psychiatry, 79*(2), 16.

Tone, E. B., and Tully, E. C. (2015). Empathy as a "risky strength": A multilevel examination of empathy and risk for internalizing disorders. *Developmental Psychopathology, 4*(2), 1547–1565.

Turner, B. J., Austin, S. B., and Chapman, A. L. (2014). Treating non-suicidal self-injury: A systematic review of psychological and pharmacological interventions. *The Canadian Journal of Psychiatry, 59*(11), 576–585.

U.S. Dept. of Education. (2018). Part B. Subpart A. Sec. 300.8 Child with a disability. Individuals with Disability. Act. Retrieved on February 10, 2021 from: Sec. 300.8 Child with a disability – Individuals with Disabilities Education Act.

Vahl, T. S., Jakubovski, E., and Müller-Vahl, K. R. (2016). New insights into clinical characteristics of Gilles de la Tourette Syndrome: Findings in 1032 patients from a single German center. *Frontiers in Neuroscience, 10*, 415.

Van Santen, J. P., Sproat, R. W., and Hill, A. P. (2013). Quantifying repetitive speech in autism spectrum disorders and language impairment. *Autism Research, 6*(5), 372–383.

Van den Bogaard, K. J., Nijman, H. L., Palmstierna, T., and Embregts, P. J. (2018). Self-injurious behavior in people with intellectual disabilities and co-occurring psychopathology using the self-harm scale: A pilot study. *Journal of Developmental and Physical Disabilities, 30*(5), 707–722.

Varnes, S. C., et al. (2006). Functional genetic analysis of mutations implicated in a human speech and language disorder. *Human Molecular Genetics, 15*(21), 3154–3167.

Werner, K. B., Few, L. R., and Bucholz, K. K. (2015). Epidemiology, comorbidity, and behavioral genetics of antisocial personality disorder and psychopathy. *Psychiatric Annals, 45*(4), 195–199.

Williams, D., Botting, N. and Boucher, J. (2008). Language in autism and specific language impairment: Where are the links? *Psychological Bulletin, 134*(6), 944–963.

Williams, M. T., Chapman, L. K., Simms, J. V., and Tellawi, G. (2017). *The Wiley handbook of obsessive-compulsive disorders (1st Ed.)*. Hoboken, NJ: John Wiley & Sons Ltd.

Wu, Y., and Hallett, M. (2017). Photophobia in neurologic disorders. *Translational Neurodegeneration, 6*(26), 1–6.

Yang, Y., Glenn, A. L., and Raine, A. (2008). Brain abnormalities in antisocial individuals: implications for the law. *Behavioral Sciences and the Law, 26*(1), 65–83.

Appendix

Section I. Approximate Locations of Parts of the Brain

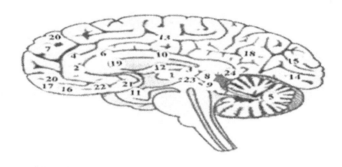

1. Amygdala
2. Anterior Cingulate Cortices
3. Basal Ganglia
4. Broca's Region
5. Cerebellum
6. Corpus Callosum
7. Frontal Cortex
8. Hippocampus
9. Hypothalamus
10. Left Posterior Cingulate
11. Left Temporal Lobe
12. Limbic System
13. Medial Temporal Lobe
14. Occipital Cortex
15. Occipital Lobe
16. Olfactory Bulb
17. Orbitofrontal
18. Parietal Region
19. Perisylvian Area
20. Prefrontal Cortex
21. Superior Temporal Gyrus
22. Temporal Lobe
23. Thalamus
24. Wernicke's Area

Match number on brain with list below to determine approximate locations.

Section II. List of Drugs Used to Treat Disabilities, Disorders, and Comorbidities

Attention Deficit Hyperactivity Disorder (ADHD)

Drug	Classification	Other Names	Side Effects
Adderall XR	S	Amphetamine	Agitation, dizziness, headache, weakness, anxiety, blurred vision, insomnia, dry mouth
Concerta	S	Methylphenidate	Insomnia, loss of appetite, weight loss, dizziness, nausea, nervousness, vomiting, or headache
Dexedrine	S	Amphetamine	Irritability, restlessness, insomnia, loss of appetite, weight loss, dizziness, nausea, nervousness, vomiting, or headache
Evekeo	S	Amphetamine	Bad taste in month, irritability, restlessness, insomnia, loss of appetite, weight loss, dizziness, nausea, nervousness, vomiting, or headache
Focalin XR	S	Dexmethylphenidate	Heart burn, dizziness, numbness/pain/skin color change, sensitivity to temperature in the fingers or toes, arrhythmia in the heartbeat, mental and mood behavior changes including agitation, aggression, mood

			swings, abnormal thoughts, thoughts of suicide
Quillivant XR	S	Methylphenidate	Irritability, restlessness, insomnia, loss of appetite, weight loss, dizziness, nausea, nervousness, vomiting, or headache
Ritalin	S	Methylphenidate	Irritability, restlessness, insomnia, loss of appetite, weight loss, dizziness, nausea, nervousness, vomiting, or headache
Strattera	N	Atomoxetine	Decreased libido or sexual side effects, feeling sleepy, sluggish, or weak during the day. Irritability, restlessness, insomnia, loss of appetite, weight loss, dizziness, nausea, nervousness, vomiting, or headache

Key
D – Depressant
N – Neither Depressant nor Stimulant
S – Stimulant

Autism Spectrum Disorder (ASD)

Drug	Classification	Other Names	Side Effects
Abilify	S	Aripripazole	Excess saliva and drooling, blurred vision, weight gain, constipation, irritability, restlessness, insomnia, loss of appetite, weight loss, dizziness, nausea, nervousness, vomiting, headache
Clozapine	D	Clozaril	Insomnia, loss of appetite, weight loss, dizziness, nausea, nervousness, vomiting, or headache, fever, increased sweating
Risperidone	S	Risperdal	Extrapyramidal effects (involuntary jerking), excess saliva and drooling, blurred vision, weight gain, constipation, irritability, restlessness, insomnia, loss of appetite, weight loss, dizziness, nausea, nervousness, vomiting, or headache, abnormal growth of breasts and glandular tissue in males
Sertraline	D	Serotonin	Irritability, restlessness, insomnia, loss of appetite, weight loss, dizziness, nausea, nervousness, vomiting, or headache

> Key
> D – Depressant
> N – Neither Depressant nor Stimulant
> S – Stimulant

Bipolar Disorder

Drug	Classification	Other Names	Side Effects
Depakote	D	Valproate	Drowsiness, change in weight, liver damage, dizziness, pancreatitis, suicidal thoughts, blood, metabolic disorders
Equetro	S	Carbamazepine	Constipation, dry mouth, weight gain, dry mouth
Lamictal	S	Lamictal ODT	Non-serious rash, restlessness, nausea, insomnia, loss of appetite, weight loss, dizziness, nervousness, vomiting, headache
Lithium	D	Benztropine	Hand tremors, restlessness, nausea, insomnia, loss of appetite, weight loss, dizziness, nervousness, vomiting, headache increased thirst
Placebo	N	No medical ingredients	None
Quetiapine	S	Seroquel	Pain in joints, indigestion, constipation,

				restlessness, nausea, insomnia, loss of appetite, weight loss, dizziness, nervousness, vomiting, headache
Tegretol		S	Carbamazepine	Swollen tongue, loss of balance, restlessness, nausea, insomnia, loss of appetite, weight loss, dizziness, nervousness, vomiting, headache
Valproic Acid		D	Convulex	Stomach pain, restlessness, nausea, insomnia, loss of appetite, weight gain, dizziness, nervousness, vomiting, headache, dry month, loss of hair

Key
D – Depressant
N – Neither Depressant nor Stimulant
S – Stimulant

Echolalia (Drugs for Comorbidities)

Drug	Classification	Other Names	Side Effects
Celexa	D	Citalopram	Headache, anxiety, perspiration, hot flashes. Tremor, nausea, vomiting, diarrhea, upset stomach, constipation
Prozac	S	Fluoxetine	For anxiety, insomnia, loss of appetite, dizziness, nausea, nervousness, vomiting, or headache, fever, increased sweating

Key
D – Depressant
N – Neither Depressant nor Stimulant
S – Stimulant

Emotional Disorder

Drug	Classification	Other Names	Side Effects
Ativan	D	Benzodiazepine	Loss of balance, nausea, insomnia, blurred vision, dizziness, headache, vomiting, muscle weakness
Buspirone	D	Namanspin	Restlessness, loss of balance, nausea, insomnia, blurred vision, dizziness,

				headache, vomiting, muscle weakness
Chlor-Trimeton	S		Antihistamine	Heart burn, dizziness, mucus thickening in the airways, arrythmia in the heartbeat, low blood pressure, blurred vision or diplopia, difficulty urinating
Norpramin	S		Desipramine	Insomnia, loss of appetite, weight loss, dizziness, nausea, nervousness, vomiting, or headache, dry mouth, constipation
Tofranil	N		Imipramine	Insomnia, loss of appetite, weight loss or gain, dizziness, nausea, sweating, vomiting, or headache, dry mouth, constipation

Key
D – Depressant
N – Neither Depressant nor Stimulant
S – Stimulant

Fetal Alcohol Syndrome Disorder (Drugs for Comorbidities)

Drug	Classification	Other Names	Side Effects
Ativan	D	Benzodiazepine	Loss of balance, nausea, insomnia, blurred vision, dizziness, headache, vomiting, muscle weakness
Norpramin	S	Desipramine	Insomnia, loss of appetite, weight loss, dizziness, nausea, nervousness, vomiting, or headache, dry mouth, constipation
Tofranil	N	Imipramine	Insomnia, loss of appetite, weight loss or gain, dizziness, nausea, sweating, vomiting, or headache, dry mouth, constipation

Key
D – Depressant
N – Neither Depressant nor Stimulant
S – Stimulant

Hyperosmia (Drugs for Comorbidities)

Drug	Classification	Other Names	Side Effects
Anesthetic spray	S	Decongestant	Difficulty breathing nausea, stinging, swelling, burning, dizziness, chest pain drowsiness, possible addiction
Oxymetazoline spray	S	Decongestant	Burning, stinging, sneezing, dizziness, chest pain, nausea drowsiness, possible addiction, nervousness

Key
D – Depressant
N – Neither Depressant nor Stimulant
S – Stimulant

Intellectual Disorder

Drug	Classification	Other Names	Side Effects
Ativan	D	Benzodiazepines	Loss of balance, nausea, insomnia, blurred vision, dizziness, headache, vomiting, muscle weakness
Celexa	D	Citalopram	Headache, anxiety, perspiration, hot flashes. Tremor, nausea, vomiting, diarrhea, upset stomach, constipation
Desyrel	D	Trazodone	Diarrhea, changes in weight, drowsiness, dizziness, tiredness, blurred vision, headache, muscle ache/pain, dry mouth, nausea, vomiting, bad taste in

			mouth, stuffy nose, constipation, or change in sexual interest/ability
Lexapro	S	Cipralex	Insomnia, loss of appetite, weight loss, dizziness, nausea, nervousness, vomiting, or headache
Prozac	S	Fluoxetine	For anxiety, insomnia, loss of appetite, dizziness, nausea, nervousness, vomiting, or headache, fever, increased sweating
Xanax	D	Benzodiazepines	Slurred speech, memory problems, insomnia, trouble concentrating, dizziness, nausea, nervousness, vomiting or headache, poor balance
Zoloft	D	Asenapine	Irritability, restlessness, insomnia, tiredness, weight loss, dizziness, nausea, nervousness, vomiting, headache, skin rash

Key
D – Depressant
N – Neither Depressant nor Stimulant
S – Stimulant

Learning Disability

Drug	Classification	Other Names	Side Effects
Lithium	D	Benztropine	Hand tremors, restlessness, nausea, insomnia, loss of appetite, weight loss, dizziness, nervousness, vomiting, headache increased thirst
Latuda	D	Lurasidone	Dizziness, nausea, lightheadedness, trepidation, weight gain, mask-like facial expression, restlessness, agitation
Metadate	S	Methylphenidate HCl	Insomnia, dizziness, nausea, stomach pain, vomiting, loss of appetite loss, weight loss, dizziness, headaches
Migraine Beta-Blockers	D	Propranolol	Cold hands or feet, feeling dizzy or tired, difficulties sleeping and nightmares.

Key
D – Depressant
N – Neither Depressant nor Stimulant
S – Stimulant

Misophonia (Drugs for Comorbidities)

Drug	Classification	Other Names	Side Effects
Ativan	D	Lorazepam	Loss of balance, nausea, insomnia, blurred vision, dizziness, headache, vomiting, muscle weakness
Buspar	D	Buspirone	Restlessness, loss of balance, nausea, insomnia, blurred vision, dizziness, headache, vomiting, muscle weakness
Klonopin	D	Benzodiazepines	Slurred speech, memory problems, insomnia, trouble concentrating, dizziness, nausea, nervousness, vomiting, or headache, poor balance
Valium	D	Benzodiazepines	Slurred speech, memory problems, insomnia, trouble concentrating, dizziness, nausea, nervousness, vomiting, or headache, poor balance
Xanax	D	Benzodiazepines	Slurred speech, memory problems, insomnia, trouble concentrating,

			dizziness, nausea, nervousness, vomiting or headache, poor balance

Key
D – Depressant
N – Neither Depressant nor Stimulant
S – Stimulant

Obsessive Compulsive Disorder

Drug	Classification	Other Names	Side Effects
Anafranil	D	Clomipramine	Dry mouth, constipation, nausea, dizziness, drowsiness, changes in appetite, blurred vision, flushing, sweating
Celexa	D	Citalopram	Headache, anxiety, perspiration, hot flashes. Tremor, nausea, vomiting, diarrhea, upset stomach, constipation
Paxil	S	Paroxetine	Weakness, dry mouth, irritability, restlessness, insomnia, loss of appetite, blurred vision, dizziness, nausea, drowsiness, dry mouth, headache
Prozac	S	Fluoxetine	For anxiety, insomnia, loss of appetite, dizziness, nausea, nervousness, vomiting,

				or headache, fever, increased sweating
Serotonin Reuptake Inhibitor (SSRI)	S		Antidepressant	Irritability, restlessness, insomnia, loss of appetite, weight loss, dizziness, nausea, nervousness, vomiting, or headache
Xanax	D		Benzodiazepines	Slurred speech, memory problems, insomnia, trouble concentrating, dizziness, nausea, nervousness, vomiting, or headache, poor balance

Key
D – Depressant
N – Neither Depressant nor Stimulant
S – Stimulant

Obsessive Defiant Disorder (ODD) (Drugs for Comorbidities)

Drug	Classification	Other Names	Side Effects
Ability	S	Aripiprazole	Allergic reactions, excess saliva and drooling, blurred vision, weight gain, constipation, irritability, restlessness, insomnia, loss of appetite, weight loss, dizziness, nausea, nervousness, vomiting, headache
Risperidone	S	Risperdal	Extrapyramidal effects (involuntary jerking), excess saliva and drooling, blurred

				vision, weight gain, constipation, irritability, restlessness, insomnia, loss of appetite, weight loss, dizziness, nausea, nervousness, vomiting or headache, abnormal growth of breasts and glandular tissue in males
Xanax	D		Benzodiazepines	Slurred speech, memory problems, insomnia, trouble concentrating, dizziness, nausea, nervousness, vomiting, or headache, poor balance

Key
D – Depressant
N – Neither Depressant nor Stimulant
S – Stimulant

Photophobia

Drug	Classification	Other Names	Side Effects
Aspirin	S	Salicylates	Nausea, vomiting, heart burn, excess acid secretion in stomach, stomach cramps, irritation in the intestines, blood thinning
Excedrin	S	Salicylates	Asthma, hives, blisters, rash, stomach ulcers, blood thinning

Ibuprofen	D		Nurofen	Nausea, vomiting, stomach pain, black feces, feeling tired or sleepy, tinnitus
Migraine Beta-Blockers	S		Propranolol	Cold hands or feet, feeling dizzy or tired, difficulties sleeping and nightmares.

Key
D – Depressant
N – Neither Depressant nor Stimulant
S – Stimulant

Rett Syndrome

Drug	Classification	Other Names	Side Effects
Lamotrigine	N	Lamictal	Non-serious rash, restlessness, nausea, insomnia, loss of appetite, weight loss, dizziness, nervousness, vomiting, headache
Levetiracetam	S	Keppra	Insomnia, dizziness, agitated, loss of strength and energy, mood swings, changes in behavior, dysphasia, loss of appetite, weight loss, headaches

Drug	Classification	Other Names	Side Effects
Oxcarbazepine	D	Trileptal	Diplopia, blurred visions, cataracts imbalance, loss of strength and energy, dizziness, nausea, vomiting, trembling
Valproic Acid	D	Depakote	Stomach pain, restlessness, nausea, insomnia, loss of appetite, weight gain, dizziness, nervousness, vomiting, headache, dry mouth, loss of hair

Key
D – Depressant
N – Neither Depressant nor Stimulant
S – Stimulant

Schizophrenia

Drug	Classification	Other Names	Side Effects
Abilify	D	Aripiprazole	Allergic reactions, excess saliva and drooling, blurred vision, weight gain, constipation, irritability, restlessness, insomnia, loss of appetite, weight loss, dizziness, nausea, nervousness, vomiting, headache
Haloperidol	D	Haldol	Allergic reaction, extrapyramidal effects (involuntary jerking), excess

				saliva and drooling, blurred vision, weight gain, constipation, irritability, restlessness, insomnia, loss of appetite, weight loss, dizziness, nausea, nervousness, vomiting, or headache, abnormal growth of breasts and glandular tissue in males
Latuda	D		Lurasidone	Dizziness, nausea, lightheadedness, trepidation, weight gain, mask-like facial expression, restlessness, agitation
Risperdal	N		Risperidone	Extrapyramidal effects (involuntary jerking), excess saliva and drooling, blurred vision, weight gain, constipation, irritability, restlessness, insomnia, loss of appetite, weight loss, dizziness, nausea, nervousness, vomiting, or headache, abnormal growth of breasts and glandular tissue in males

Key
D – Depressant
N – Neither Depressant nor Stimulant
S – Stimulant

Self-Injurious Behavior

Drug	Classification	Other Names	Side Effects
Abilify	D	Aripiprazole	Allergic reactions, excess saliva and drooling, blurred vision, weight gain, constipation, irritability, restlessness, insomnia, loss of appetite, weight loss, dizziness, nausea, nervousness, vomiting, headache
Celexa	D	Haldol	Headache, anxiety, perspiration, hot flashes. Tremor, nausea, vomiting, diarrhea, upset stomach, constipation
Carbamazepine	S	Equetro	Constipation, dry mouth, weight gain, dry mouth
Clozaril	D	Lurasidone	Insomnia, loss of appetite, weight loss, dizziness, nausea, nervousness, vomiting, or headache, fever, increased sweating
Depakote	D	Valproate	Drowsiness, change in weight, liver damage, dizziness, pancreatitis, suicidal thoughts, blood, metabolic disorders
Depakene	D	Valproate	Drowsiness, change in weight, liver damage, dizziness,

				pancreatitis, suicidal thoughts, blood, metabolic disorders
Lamotrigine	N		Lamictal	Non-serious rash, restlessness, nausea, insomnia, loss of appetite, weight loss, dizziness, nervousness, vomiting, headache
Lithium	D		Benztropine	Hand tremors, restlessness, nausea, insomnia, loss of appetite, weight loss, dizziness, nervousness, vomiting, headache increased thirst
Paxil	S		Paroxetine	Weakness, dry mouth, irritability, restlessness, insomnia, loss of appetite, blurred vision, dizziness, nausea, drowsiness, dry mouth, headache
Prozac	S		Fluoxetine	For anxiety, insomnia, loss of appetite, dizziness, nausea, nervousness, vomiting, or headache, fever, increased sweating
Risperdal	N		Risperidone	Extrapyramidal effects (involuntary jerking), excess saliva and drooling, blurred vision, weight gain, constipation, irritability, restlessness, insomnia, loss of appetite, weight loss, dizziness, nausea, nervousness, vomiting, or headache, abnormal

Drug				Side Effects
				growth of breasts and glandular tissue in males
Zoloft	S		Asenapine	Irritability, restlessness, insomnia, tiredness, weight loss, dizziness, nausea, nervousness, vomiting, headache, skin rash

Key
D – Depressant
N – Neither Depressant nor Stimulant
S – Stimulant

Antisocial Personality Disorder

Drug	Classification	Other Names	Side Effects
Amantadine	S	Gocovri	Allergic reactions
Bromocriptine	S	Cycloset	Dizziness, nausea, diarrhea, vomiting, loss of appetite, weight loss, headaches, constipation
Desipramine	S	Norpramin	Insomnia, loss of appetite, weight loss, dizziness, nausea, nervousness, vomiting, or headache, dry mouth, constipation
Nortriptyline	S	Pamelor	Anxiety, weakness, tiredness, nausea, diarrhea, vomiting, changes in appetite, changes in

Drug	Classification	Other Names	Side Effects
			weight, headaches, constipation, dry mouth, drowsiness
Phenytoin	D	Dilantin	Nervousness, trepidation, weakness, tiredness, nausea, diarrhea, vomiting, changes in appetite, changes in weight, headaches, constipation, dry mouth, drowsiness, sore or swollen gums, skin rash

Key
D – Depressant
N – Neither Depressant nor Stimulant
S – Stimulant

Social Skill Deficits and Speech/Language Disorder (Drugs for Comorbidities)

Drug	Classification	Other Names	Side Effects
Abilify	D	Aripiprazole	Allergic reactions, excess saliva and drooling, blurred vision, weight gain, constipation, irritability, restlessness, insomnia, loss of appetite, weight loss, dizziness, nausea, nervousness, vomiting, headache
Haloperidol	D	Haldol	Allergic reactions, extrapyramidal effects (involuntary jerking), excess saliva and drooling, blurred

			vision, weight gain, constipation, irritability, restlessness, insomnia, loss of appetite, weight loss, dizziness, nausea, nervousness, vomiting, or headache, abnormal growth of breasts and glandular tissue in males
Risperdal	N	Risperidone	Extrapyramidal effects (involuntary jerking), excess saliva and drooling, blurred vision, weight gain, constipation, irritability, restlessness, insomnia, loss of appetite, weight loss, dizziness, nausea, nervousness, vomiting, or headache, abnormal growth of breasts and glandular tissue in males
Saphris	S	Asenapine	Irritability, restlessness, insomnia, tiredness, weight loss, dizziness, nausea, nervousness, vomiting, headache, skin rash

Key
D – Depressant
N – Neither Depressant nor Stimulant
S – Stimulant

Tourette Syndrome

Drug	Classification	Other Names	Side Effects
Fluphenazine	D	Modecate	Anxiety, upset stomach, trepidation, nightmares, skin sensitive to sunlight, changes in appetite, changes in weight, dry mouth, drowsiness, sore or swollen gums, skin rash
Haloperidol	D	Haldol	Allergic reactions, extrapyramidal effects (involuntary jerking), excess saliva and drooling, blurred vision, weight gain, constipation, irritability, restlessness, insomnia, loss of appetite, weight loss, dizziness, nausea, nervousness, vomiting or headache, abnormal growth of breasts and glandular tissue in males
Pimozide	D	Orap	Increased hunger or thirst, dizziness, nausea, nervousness, vomiting, or headache, diarrhea, constipation, increased saliva, changes in posture
Risperdal	N	Asenapine	Extrapyramidal effects (involuntary jerking), excess saliva and drooling, blurred vision, weight gain, constipation, irritability, restlessness, insomnia,

			loss of appetite, weight loss, dizziness, nausea, nervousness, vomiting, or headache, abnormal growth of breasts and glandular tissue in males

Key
D – Depressant
N – Neither Depressant nor Stimulant
S – Stimulant

Indexs

A

Abuse 21, 62, 70
73, 89, 93, 94, 96
Academic Progress 30, 51, 56
58, 59, 60, 63, 85, 87, 108, 114
Acceptable Classroom Practice 47
Accommodations 33, 58, 63, 68
ADHD 22, 27, 31, 41
42, 43, 45, 49, 51, 53, 55
57, 58, 59, 61, 63, 66, 68, 71, 74
76, 77, 93, 96, 99, 101, 104
106, 110, 115, 120, 121, 123, 134
Aggression 43, 60, 61, 71, 72, 96
Aggressive 30, 31, 95
Agitation 33, 88, 134, 144, 151
Amygdala 49, 61, 71
72, 89, 93, 110
Anger 21, 22, 61, 88
animal assisted therapy 54
anterior cingulate cortex 94
anterior cingulate cortices 67
Antisocial Personality
Disorder 89, 92, 93
Anxiety 21, 31, 33, 40
42, 43, 46, 48, 50, 53, 54
55, 62, 65, 67, 72, 76, 85, 91
94, 96, 105, 106, 114, 125
134, 139, 142, 143, 146, 152

Applied Behavior Analysis 22, 23
27, 36, 54, 62, 108
argumentative 70, 73
ASD 25, 27, 29, 31, 37
38, 39, 41, 43, 45, 49, 50, 51
52, 53, 55, 57, 59, 61, 63, 65
66, 68, 71, 74, 76, 79, 80
87, 88, 90, 97, 98, 101, 115
Asperger's Disorder 83
Autism 25, 28, 35, 38, 42, 46
49, 53, 79, 83, 110
117, 119, 121, 123, 131

B

Baker Act 86, 123
Basal Ganglia 45, 67, 104
Behavioral Meltdowns 34
Behavioral Strategies 46
Behavioralists 32, 57, 90
BIP 58
Bipolar Disorder 31, 32
Brain 20, 26, 27, 30, 32, 35
36, 37, 41, 42, 44, 48
53, 57, 61, 66, 67, 70, 75, 79
82, 85, 90, 92, 94, 98, 104
110, 111, 112, 115, 116, 118
Brain Damage 44

Brain Size 44
Broca area 99
Broca's Region 57, 110
Comorbid 62, 83, 85, 96
98, 108, 123

C
ADHD 20, 22, 31, 61, 63, 68
74, 93, 96, 99, 106
110, 115, 120, 121
ASD 25, 26, 29, 36, 59
63, 68, 76, 83, 87, 98, 101
Catatonic Schizophrenia 84
Cerebellum 27, 45, 111
Changes in Mood 30
Classroom Interventions 33
Classroom Management 38
50, 51, 54, 62, 63, 74
77, 102, 105, 106
cognitive disfunctions 56
Cognitive-Behavioral Therapy 41
62
Comorbid 41, 45, 65, 68
Comorbidities 21, 45
Corpus Callosum 45
counterconditioning 61, 72

D
defiant 70, 73, 115, 126, 130
Delayed Development 44
delusional 83, 87, 93
delusions 83, 84, 85, 117
Depressive Disorder 61
Developmental Disability 25
developmental social
pragmatic therapy 54

Dialectical behavior therapy 61
Differential Reinforcement 37
Differentiated 28, 54
discipline 70
Discomfort 48, 49, 75
88, 116, 118
disconnected from reality 84
DSM-5 30, 70, 84, 112
Dyscalculia 56, 57, 111
Dyslexia 57, 59, 112, 126

E
Echolalia 36, 112, 124, 130
ED 40, 42
Electroconvulsive Therapy 86
Emapathize 52
emotional evocation 88
Empathize 92
Environmental 21, 26, 48
56, 70, 84, 93, 120, 123, 130
Evidence-Based Practices 23
29, 30, 33, 34, 38, 39, 40, 43, 46
68, 69, 78, 82, 91, 96, 97, 100, 101

F
Fake drugs 73
false sensory perceptions 84
FASD 44, 113
Fetal Alcohol Syndrome 44, 52
99, 113, 126
Frontal Cortex 32
frontal lobe 57, 111, 113

G
General Education Teachers 29
Genes 20, 103, 113

Genetic   20, 22, 25, 38, 41, 48, 49
Genetic Disorder   25, 52
   87, 90, 91, 98, 113

H
hallucinations   58, 83, 84, 85, 113
Hallucinatory   84
hallucinatory behaviors   84
Heredity   21, 92, 113, 117
Hippocampus   25, 27, 45
   49, 89, 113
Hyperactivity   20, 27, 41, 57
   84, 110, 121, 122, 123, 128
Hyperosmia   48, 49, 113, 124
Hyperprolactinemia   72, 114
hypothalamus   114

I
ID   52, 54
IEP   34, 45, 58, 91, 106
Impulsive Behavior   20, 110
Inability to Learn   40
Inappropriate Behavior   18, 22, 32
   33, 42, 60, 74, 88, 89, 100, 105
Individualized Education Plan   45
   114

J
Judgment   45, 52, 62, 111

L
LD   53, 56, 58, 59
Learning Styles   23, 28, 58, 130
left posterior cingulate cortex   89
limbic system   110, 114

M
ADHD   21
ASD   71, 74, 91, 97
Maladaptive Behaviors   40, 43
Manic-Depressive
Mental Illness   30
Manipulatives   54, 81
Medications   22, 24, 50, 51
   58, 61, 65, 72, 75, 79, 85, 90, 95
Memory   52, 57, 111
   113, 115, 143, 147
Misophonia   60, 61, 62
   114, 117, 122, 123, 128
Mood stabilizers   32, 90
Mood Swings   30, 32, 34, 135
motor skills   56, 80, 81, 113
Multi-Disciplinary
Evaluation Team   58, 63, 114
Multiple Intelligences   23, 54, 115

N
neglect   70, 92
nervous system disorder   103, 106
neurobiological variances   70
neurodevelopmental disorder   103
   104, 110
Neurological Disorder   29
neurophysiological   61
noises and sounds   61
number sense   57, 112
neurodevelopmental disorder   115

O
occipital cortex   80
occipital lobe   53
OCD   61, 65, 66, 67

	68, 70, 85, 87, 106, 115
ODD	70, 72, 88, 91, 99
	100, 104, 115, 120, 147
Olfactory Bulb	49
orbitofrontal	67

P

Antisocial Personality Disorders	92
paranoid Schizophrenia	84
Parietal Regions	32
PDD-NOS	66, 83, 116
perisylvian	57
pervasive developmental Disorder	83, 116
Photophobia	75, 76, 116, 132
Placebo	33
Prefrontal	21, 72, 85, 94, 99, 115
prefrontal cortex	21, 72
	94, 99, 115, 116
Prefrontal Cortex region	99
Professional Awareness	46
Professional Development	47
	51, 55, 59, 63, 68, 73, 74, 82, 87
psychiatric disorder	35, 66
psychiatrist	85
Psychological Intervention	41
psychologist	28, 30, 38
	42, 54, 85, 90, 91
Psychopathological Disorder	40
	112
Psychopathology	92, 95
Psychopaths	92, 96
psychosocial	49, 85, 87, 130
psychosocial treatments	85
psychotherapy	32, 41, 42

	43, 55, 62, 67, 68, 72, 74
	76, 82, 88, 94, 105, 111, 117
Psychotic Disorders	21, 40, 41
psychotropic drugs	54

R

Reasoning	45, 52, 117
Repetition	35, 36, 46, 101, 112, 117
Repetitive Behaviors	25, 65
Rett Syndrome	79, 117

S

Antisocial Personality Disorder,	92
Evidence-Based Practices	23
Schizophrenia	36, 38, 66, 68
	71, 74, 83, 85, 96, 112, 115, 129
School Psychologists	32, 54, 55, 90
School Social Workers	42
Scientific-Based Methods	23, 28
Seizures	41, 58, 76, 80, 81
Self-Injurious Behavior	41, 68
	88, 89, 117
Sensory Disorder	48, 51, 55
	60, 75, 116
Smaller Brain	45
Smell	48, 84, 113
Social Anxiety Disorder	85
Social Development	100
Social Disorders	41, 43
Social Pathology	92, 118
Social Paths	93, 118
Social Skill Deficits	27, 45
	59, 98, 100, 101, 118
Social Skills Deficits	85, 87
Speech/Language Deficit	41
	43, 57

Speech/Language Disorders 87, 88, 89
speech-language therapist pathologist 85
stimulus substitution 62
Student Meltdowns 18, 77
substance abuse 62
Succinct 28, 33, 42, 46, 50, 54, 98

T
ADHD 63, 93
ASD 25
Tactile Learners 23, 28
Teaching Strategies 23, 29, 37, 42
Temporal 32, 36, 53, 57, 85, 94, 99, 113, 114
thalamus 67, 76, 90, 118
Therapists 38, 42, 45, 54, 55, 57, 81, 82, 96, 100
Therapy 22, 30, 32, 33, 36, 38, 42, 43, 46, 49, 53, 55, 57, 59, 61, 63, 67, 72, 77, 81, 85, 86, 89, 90, 91, 94, 96, 97, 101, 111
Tourette Syndrome 35, 104, 105, 121
Tourette's Syndrome 103, 105, 118
Traits of ADHD 21
traumatic brain injury 62, 75, 116
Trichotillomania 66

U
UbD 33, 55, 78, 101
UDL 33, 55, 78, 101
Unchanging Routine 46
unsuitable inattention 110

W
Wernicke area 99
Wernicke's Area 36, 57
Withdrawal 41, 43, 80

CPSIA information can be obtained
at www.ICGtesting.com
Printed in the USA
BVHW051953050623
665421BV00006B/123